Modern Critical Interpretations
Thomas Hardy's
The Mayor of Casterbridge

Modern Critical Interpretations

These and other titles in preparation

Thomas Hardy's

The Mayor of Casterbridge

Edited and with an introduction by
Harold Bloom
Sterling Professor of the Humanities
Yale University

Chelsea House Publishers ◊ *1988*
NEW YORK ◊ NEW HAVEN ◊ PHILADELPHIA

© 1988 by Chelsea House Publishers, a division
of Chelsea House Educational Communications, Inc.,
  345 Whitney Avenue, New Haven, CT 06511
  95 Madison Avenue, New York, NY 10016
  5068B West Chester Pike, Edgemont, PA 19028

Introduction © 1987 by Harold Bloom

Printed and bound in the United States of America

10 9 8 7 6 5 4 3 2 1

∞ The paper used in this publication meets the minimum
requirements of the American National Standard for Permanence
of Paper for Printed Library Materials, Z39.48–1984.

Library of Congress Cataloging-in-Publication Data
Thomas Hardy's The Mayor of Casterbridge / edited and with an
introduction by Harold Bloom.
  p. cm.—(Modern critical interpretations)
  Bibliography: p.
  Includes index.
  Summary: A collection of six critical essays on the Hardy novel,
arranged in chronological order of their original publication.
  ISBN 0–87754–742–4 (alk. paper): $24.50
  1. Hardy, Thomas, 1840–1928. Mayor of Casterbridge. [1. Hardy,
Thomas, 1840–1928. Mayor of Casterbridge. 2. English literature-
-History and criticism.] I. Bloom, Harold. II. Series.
PR4750.M3T48 1988   87–15900
823'.8—dc19   CIP
                                                   AC

Contents

Editor's Note

This book brings together a representative selection of the best modern critical interpretations of Thomas Hardy's tragic novel, *The Mayor of Casterbridge.* The critical essays are reprinted here in the chronological order of their original publication. I am grateful to Christina Büchmann for her assistance in editing this volume.

My introduction considers Michael Henchard as a tragic hero, in the ancient sense of *ethos* being the *daimon,* character being fate. Bert G. Hornback begins the chronological sequence of criticism with his estimate that *The Mayor of Casterbridge* is Hardy's masterpiece, particularly in its creation of a metaphoric atmosphere dominated by chance.

The separation between Henchard's public and private history, between work and love, is studied by Ian Gregor, after which the feminist critic Elaine Showalter finds in Henchard a remarkable fusion of male rebellion and female suffering.

George Levine sees realism as surviving in Hardy's *Mayor* not as a mode for writing fiction but as a hard discipline emerging from human self-thwarted energies in the hostile context of nature. Somewhat complementary is Bruce Johnson's vision of Hardy's cosmos in this novel as a kind of ontological spinning wheel.

In this volume's final essay, J. B. Bullen traces correspondences between Thomas Carlyle's clothes metaphor in *Sartor Resartus* and a similar metaphor that pervades *The Mayor of Casterbridge,* in order to suggest affinities in how Carlyle and Hardy bring together visual appearances and psychological realities.

Introduction

For Arthur Schopenhauer, the Will to Live was the true thing-in-itself, not an interpretation but a rapacious, active, universal, and ultimately indifferent drive or desire. Schopenhauer's great work, *The World as Will and Representation,* had the same relation to and influence upon many of the principal nineteenth- and early twentieth-century novelists that Freud's writings have in regard to many of this century's later, crucial masters of prose fiction. Zola, Maupassant, Turgenev, and Tolstoy join Thomas Hardy as Schopenhauer's nineteenth-century heirs, in a tradition that goes on through Proust, Conrad, and Thomas Mann to culminate in aspects of Borges and of Beckett, the most eminent living writer of narrative. Since Schopenhauer (despite Freud's denials) was one of Freud's prime precursors, one could argue that aspects of Freud's influence upon writers simply carry on from Schopenhauer's previous effect. Manifestly, the relation of Schopenhauer to Hardy is different in both kind and degree from the larger sense in which Schopenhauer was Freud's forerunner or Wittgenstein's. A poet-novelist like Hardy turns to a rhetorical speculator like Schopenhauer only because he finds something in his own temperament and sensibility confirmed and strengthened, and not at all as Lucretius turned to Epicurus, or as Whitman was inspired by Emerson.

The true precursor for Hardy was Shelley, whose visionary skepticism permeates the novels as well as the poems and *The Dynasts.* There is some technical debt to George Eliot in the early novels, but Hardy in his depths was little more moved by her than by Wilkie Collins, from whom he also learned elements of craft. Shelley's tragic sense of eros is pervasive throughout Hardy, and ultimately determines Hardy's understanding of his strongest heroines: Bathsheba Everdene, Eustacia Vye, Marty South, Tess Durbeyfield, Sue Bridehead. Between desire and fulfillment in Shelley falls the shadow of the selfhood, a shadow that makes love and what might be called the means of love quite irreconcilable. What M. D. Zabel named as "the aesthetic of incongruity" in Hardy and ascribed to temperamental causes is in a profound way the result of attempting to transmute the procedures of *The Revolt of Islam* and *Epipsychidion* into the supposedly naturalistic novel.

J. Hillis Miller, when he worked more in the mode of a critic of consciousness like Georges Poulet than in the deconstruction of Paul de Man and Jacques Derrida, saw the fate of love in Hardy as being darkened always by a shadow cast by the lover's consciousness itself. Hugh Kenner, with a distaste for Hardy akin to (and perhaps derived from) T. S. Eliot's in *After Strange Gods,* suggested that Miller had created a kind of Proustian Hardy, who turns out to be a case rather than an artist. Hardy was certainly not an artist comparable to Henry James (who dismissed him as a mere imitator of George Eliot) or James Joyce, but the High Modernist shibboleths for testing the novel have now waned considerably, except for a few surviving high priests of Modernism like Kenner. A better guide to Hardy's permanent strength as a novelist was his heir D. H. Lawrence, whose *The Rainbow* and *Women in Love* marvelously brought Hardy's legacy to an apotheosis. Lawrence, praising Hardy with a rebel son's ambivalence, associated him with Tolstoy as a tragic writer:

> And this is the quality Hardy shares with the great writers, Shakespeare or Sophocles or Tolstoi, this setting behind the small action of his protagonists the terrific action of unfathomed nature; setting a smaller system of morality, the one grasped and formulated by the human consciousness within the vast, uncomprehended and incomprehensible morality of nature or of life itself, surpassing human consciousness. The difference is, that whereas in Shakespeare or Sophocles the greater, uncomprehended morality, or fate, is actively transgressed and gives active punishment, in Hardy and Tolstoi the lesser, human morality, the mechanical system is actively transgressed, and holds, and punishes the protagonist, whilst the greater morality is only passively, negatively transgressed, it is represented merely as being present in background, in scenery, not taking any active part, having no direct connexion with the protagonist. Œdipus, Hamlet, Macbeth set themselves up against, or find themselves set

up against, the unfathomed moral forces of nature, and out of this unfathomed force comes their death. Whereas Anna Karenina, Eustacia, Tess, Sue, and Jude find themselves up against the established system of human government and morality, they cannot detach themselves, and are brought down. Their real tragedy is that they are unfaithful to the greater unwritten morality, which would have bidden Anna Karenina be patient and wait until she, by virtue of greater right, could take what she needed from society; would have bidden Vronsky detach himself from the system, become an individual, creating a new colony of morality with Anna; would have bidden Eustacia fight Clym for his own soul, and Tess take and claim her Angel, since she had the greater light; would have bidden Jude and Sue endure for very honour's sake, since one must bide by the best that one has known, and not succumb to the lesser good.

("Study of Thomas Hardy")

This seems to me powerful and just, because it catches what is most surprising and enduring in Hardy's novels—the sublime stature and aesthetic dignity of his crucial protagonists—while exposing also his great limitation, his denial of freedom to his best personages. Lawrence's prescription for what would have saved Eustacia and Clym, Tess and Angel, Sue and Jude, is perhaps not as persuasive. He speaks of them as though they were Gudrun and Gerald, and thus have failed to be Ursula and Birkin. It is Hardy's genius that they are what they had to be: as imperfect as their creator and his vision, as impure as his language and his plotting, and finally painful and memorable to us:

> Note that, in this bitterness, delight,
> Since the imperfect is so hot in us,
> Lies in flawed words and stubborn sounds.

II

Of Hardy's major novels, *The Mayor of Casterbridge* is the least flawed and clearly the closest to tragic convention in Western literary tradition. If one hesitates to prefer it to *The Return of the Native, Tess,* or *Jude,* that may be because it is the least original and eccentric work of the four. Henchard is certainly the best articulated and most consistent of Hardy's male personages, but Lucetta is no Eustacia, and the amiable Elizabeth-Jane does not compel much of the reader's interest. The book's glory, Henchard, is so massive a self-punisher that he can be said to leap over the psychic cosmos of Schopenhauer directly into that of Freud's great essay on the economics of masochism, with its grim new category of "moral masochism." In a surprising way, Hardy reverses, through Henchard, one of the principal *topoi* of Western tragedy, as set forth acutely by Northrop Frye:

> A strong element of demonic ritual in public punishments and similar mob amusements is exploited by tragic and ironic myth. Breaking on the wheel becomes Lear's wheel of fire; bear-baiting is an image for Gloucester and Macbeth, and for the crucified Prometheus the humiliation of exposure, the horror of being watched, is a greater misery than the pain. *Derkou theama* (behold the spectacle; get your staring over with) is his bitterest cry. The inability of Milton's blind Samson to stare back is his greatest torment, and one which forces him to scream at Delilah, in one of the most terrible passages of all tragic drama, that he will tear her to pieces if she touches him.

For Henchard "the humiliation of exposure" becomes a terrible passion, until at last he makes an exhibition of himself during a royal visit. Perhaps he can revert to what Frye calls "the horror of being watched" only when he knows that the gesture involved will be his last. Hence his Will, which may be the most powerful prose passage that Hardy ever wrote:

> They stood in silence while he ran into the cottage; returning in a moment with a crumpled scrap of paper. On it there was pencilled as follows:—
>
> "MICHAEL HENCHARD'S WILL
>
> "That Elizabeth-Jane Farfrae be not told of my death, or made to grieve on account of me.
> "& that I be not bury'd in consecrated ground.
> "& that no sexton be asked to toll the bell.
> "& that nobody is wished to see my dead body.
> "& that no murners walk behind me at my funeral.
> "& that no flours be planted on my grave.
> "& that no man remember me.
> "To this I put my name.
>
> "Michael Henchard."

That dark testament is the essence of Henchard. It is notorious that "tragedy" becomes a very problematical form in the European Enlightenment and afterwards. Romanticism, which has been our continuous Modernism from the mid-1740s to the present moment, did not return the tragic hero to us, though from Richardson's Clarissa Harlowe until now we have received many resurgences of the tragic heroine. Hardy and Ibsen can be judged to have come closest to reviving the tragic hero, in contradistinction to the hero-villain who, throughout Romantic tradition, limns his night-piece and judges it to have been his best. Henchard, despite his blind strength and his terrible errors, is no villain, and as readers we suffer with him, unrelievedly, because our sympathy for him is unimpeded.

Unfortunately, the suffering becomes altogether *too* unrelieved, as it does again with Jude Fawley. Rereading *The Mayor of Casterbridge* is less painful than rereading *Jude the Obscure,* since at least we do not have to contemplate little Father Time hanging the other urchins and himself, but it is still very painful indeed. Whether or not tragedy should possess some catharsis, we resent the imposition of too much pathos upon us, and we need some gesture of purification if only to keep us away from our own defensive ironies. Henchard, alas, *accomplishes nothing,* for himself or for others. Ahab, a great hero-villain, goes down fighting his implacable fate, the whiteness of the whale, but Henchard is a self-destroyer to no purpose. And yet we are vastly moved by him and know that we should be. Why?

The novel's full title is *The Life and Death of the Mayor of Casterbridge: A Story of a Man of Character.* As Robert Louis Stevenson said in a note to Hardy, "Henchard is a great fellow," which implies that he is a great personality rather than a man of character. This is, in fact, how Hardy represents Henchard, and the critic R. H. Hutton was right to be puzzled by Hardy's title, in a review published in *The Spectator* on June 5, 1886:

> Mr. Hardy has not given us any more powerful study than that of Michael Henchard. Why he should especially term his hero in his title-page a "man of character," we do not clearly understand. Properly speaking, character is the stamp graven on a man, and character therefore, like anything which can be graven, and which, when graven, remains, is a word much more applicable to that which has fixity and permanence, than to that which is fitful and changeful, and which impresses a totally different image of itself on the

wax of plastic circumstance at one time, from that which it impresses on a similarly plastic surface at another time. To keep strictly to the associations from which the word "character" is derived, a man of character ought to suggest a man of steady and unvarying character, a man who conveys very much the same conception of his own qualities under one set of circumstances, which he conveys under another. This is true of many men, and they might be called men of character *par excellence.* But the essence of Michael Henchard is that he is a man of large nature and depth of passion, who is yet subject to the most fitful influences, who can do in one mood acts of which he will never cease to repent in almost all his other moods, whose temper of heart changes many times even during the execution of the same purpose, though the same ardour, the same pride, the same wrathful magnanimity, the same inability to carry out in cool blood the angry resolve of the mood of revenge or scorn, the same hasty unreasonableness, and the same disposition to swing back to an equally hasty reasonableness, distinguish him throughout. In one very good sense, the great deficiency of Michael Henchard might be said to be in "character." It might well be said that with a little *more* character, with a little more fixity of mind, with a little more power of recovering *himself* when he was losing his balance, his would have been a nature of gigantic mould; whereas, as Mr. Hardy's novel is meant to show, it was a nature which ran mostly to waste. But, of course, in the larger and wider sense of the word "character," that sense which has less reference to the permanent definition of the stamp, and more reference to the confidence with which the varying moods may be anticipated, it is not inadmissible to call Michael Henchard a "man of character." Still, the words on the title-page rather mislead. One looks for the picture of a man of much more constancy of purpose, and much less tragic mobility of mood, than Michael Henchard. None the less, the picture is a very vivid one, and almost magnificent in its fullness of expression. The largeness of his nature, the unreasonable generosity and suddenness of his friendships, the depth of his self-humiliation for what was evil in him, the eagerness of his craving for sympathy, the vehemence of his impulses both for good and evil, the curious dash of stoicism in a nature so eager for sympathy, and of fortitude in one so moody and restless,—all these are lineaments which, mingled together as Mr. Hardy has mingled them, produce a curiously strong impression of reality, as well as of homely grandeur.

One can summarize Hutton's point by saying that Henchard is stronger in pathos than in ethos, and yet ethos is the daimon, character is fate, and Hardy specifically sets out to show that Henchard's character is his fate. The strength of Hardy's irony is that it is also life's irony, and will become Sigmund Freud's irony: Henchard's destiny demonstrates that there are no accidents, meaning that nothing happens to one that is not already oneself. Henchard stares out at the night as though he were staring at an adversary, but there is nothing out there. There is only the self turned against the self, only the drive, beyond the pleasure principle, to death.

The pre-Socratic aphorism that character is fate seems to have been picked up by Hardy from George Eliot's *The Mill on the Floss,* where it is attributed to Novalis. But Hardy need not have gleaned it from anywhere in particular. Everyone in Hardy's novels is overdetermined by his or her past, because for Hardy, as for Freud, everything that is dreadful has already happened and there never can be anything absolutely new. Such a speculation belies the very word "novel," and certainly was no aid to Hardy's inventiveness. Nothing that happens to Henchard surprises us. His fate is redeemed from dreariness only by its aesthetic dignity, which returns us to the problematical question of Hardy's relation to tragedy as a literary form.

Henchard is burdened neither with wisdom nor with knowledge; he is a man of will and of action, with little capacity for reflection, but with a spirit perpetually open and generous towards others. J. Hillis Miller sees him as being governed erotically by mediated desire, but since Miller sees this as the iron law in Hardy's erotic universe, it loses any particular force as an observation upon Henchard. I would prefer to say that Henchard, more even than most men and like all women in Hardy, is hungry for love, desperate for some company in the void of existence. D. H. Lawrence read the tragedy of Hardy's figures not as the consequence of mediated desire, but as the fate of any desire that will not be bounded by convention and community.

This is the tragedy of Hardy, always the same: the tragedy of those who, more or less pioneers, have died in the wilderness, whither they had escaped for free action, after having left the walled security, and the comparative imprisonment, of the established convention. This is the theme of novel after novel: remain quite within the convention, and you are good, safe, and happy in the long run, though you never have the vivid pang of sympathy on your side: or, on the other hand, be passionate, individual, wilful, you will find the security of the convention a walled prison, you will escape, and you will die, either of your own lack of strength to bear the isolation and the exposure, or by direct revenge from the community, or from both. This is the tragedy, and only this: it is nothing more metaphysical than the division of a man against himself in such a way: first, that he is a member of the community, and must, upon his honour, in no way move to disintegrate the community, either in its moral or its practical form; second, that the convention of the community is a prison to his natural, individual desire, a desire that compels him, whether he feel justified or not, to break the bounds of the community, lands him outside the pale, there to stand alone, and say: "I was right, my desire was real and inevitable; if I was to be myself I must fulfil it, convention or no convention," or else, there to stand alone, doubting, and saying: "Was I right, was I wrong? If I was wrong, oh, let me die!"—in which case he courts death.

The growth and the development of this tragedy, the deeper and deeper realisation of this division and this problem, the coming towards some conclusion, is the one theme of the Wessex novels.

("Study of Thomas Hardy")

This is general enough to be just, but not quite specific enough for the self-destructive Henchard. Also not sufficiently specific is the sympathetic judgment of Irving Howe, who speaks of "Henchard's personal struggle—the struggle of a splendid animal trying to escape a trap and thereby entangling itself all the more." I find more precise the dark musings of Sigmund Freud, Hardy's contemporary, who might be thinking of Michael Henchard when he meditates upon "The Economic Problem in Masochism":

The third form of masochism, the moral type, is chiefly remarkable for having loosened its connection with what we recognize to be sexuality. To all other masochistic sufferings there still clings the condition that it should be administered by the loved person; it is endured at his command; in the moral type of masochism this limitation has been dropped. It is the suffering itself that matters; whether the sentence is cast by a loved or by an indifferent person is of no importance; it may even be caused by impersonal forces or circumstances, but the true masochist always holds out his cheek wherever he sees a chance of receiving a blow.

The origins of "moral masochism" are in an unconscious sense of guilt, a need for punishment that transcends actual culpability. Even Henchard's original and grotesque "crime," his drunken exploit in wife-selling, does not so much engender in him remorse at the consciousness of wrongdoing, but rather helps engulf him in the "guilt" of the moral masochist. That means Henchard knows his guilt not as affect or emotion but as a negation, as the nullification of his desires and his ambitions. In a more than Freudian sense, Henchard's primal ambivalence is directed against himself, against the authority principle in his own self.

If *The Mayor of Casterbridge* is a less original book than *Tess* or *Jude,* it is also a more persuasive and universal vision than Hardy achieved elsewhere. Miguel de Unamuno, defining the tragic sense of life, remarked that: "The chiefest sanctity of a temple is that it is a place to which men go to weep in common. A *miserere* sung in common by a multitude tormented by destiny has as much value as a philosophy." That is not tragedy as Aristotle defined it, but it is tragedy as Thomas Hardy wrote it.

The Metaphor of Chance:
The Mayor of Casterbridge

Bert G. Hornback

> *"Casterbridge is a old, hoary place o' wickedness, by all account. 'Tis recorded in history that we rebelled against the King one or two hundred years ago, in the time of the Romans."*
>
> The Mayor of Casterbridge

Hardy's 1895-1912 preface to *The Mayor of Casterbridge* notes that, "The incidents narrated arise mainly out of three events, which chanced to range themselves in the order and at or about the intervals of time here given, in the real history of the town called Casterbridge and in the neighbouring country. They were the sale of a wife by her husband, the uncertain harvests which immediately preceded the repeal of the Corn Laws, and the visit of a Royal personage to the aforesaid part of England." There are but five characters drawn in detail for the acting out of this seemingly simple story, and four of them serve primarily to involve and entangle the fifth. Hardy called the novel "more particularly a study of one man's deeds and character than, perhaps, any other of those included in my Exhibition of Wessex life." Michael Henchard, the one "Man of Character," is supported and crossed at every turn by Susan, Elizabeth-Jane, Farfrae, and Lucetta. And he is interfered with by the furmity-woman, by the local chorus of rustics, and by his own private Fedullah, Joshua Jopp. His career, thus involved and complicated, is the plot of the novel. He sells his wife, loses all he has misguessing the harvest, and is publicly disgraced at the visit of the Royal personage.

From *The Metaphor of Chance: Vision and Technique in the Works of Thomas Hardy.* ©1971 by Bert G. Hornback. Ohio University Press, 1971.

Hardy's problem is how to make Michael Henchard larger than he is as the mayor of a small country town. The novel belongs strictly and almost entirely to Henchard: its full title is *The Life and Death of The Mayor of Casterbridge: A Story of a Man of Character.* Though his term as mayor is over in chapter 27 and his title is taken soon thereafter by Donald Farfrae, still he remains mayor—as Lear remains King. But being mayor—or King—is not enough. Nor is it enough for Hardy that Henchard stands as symbol for the passing of an age in England's history, for this makes him neither Oedipan nor of a kind and size with Lear. Hardy's plot for Henchard stresses his tragic fault, as his one mistake keeps returning to haunt him throughout his life; but this alone does not make the story of his fall great drama, or tragedy, even if we call him always "a Man of Character." Henchard's existence is not an intellectual one, either, for the sensitive critical vision is given to Elizabeth-Jane. Henchard's awareness is limited to himself and that immediate world in which he strives, not only for survival, but for the dignity of a man free to meet his fate. It is in achieving this freedom that he becomes, legitimately, "a Man of Character," that he makes himself significantly "The Mayor," that he becomes the novel's hero.

Henchard grows always toward this size throughout the novel. In *The Return of the Native* a stage for universally representative action is constructed overtly at the beginning of the novel, and the stage almost outsizes the characters who are asked to live up to its demands. In *The Mayor of Casterbridge* Hardy is much more subtle, and takes his time about building both the stage and the character to fit it. He exercises what Albert Guerard would call his "tact" in the use of his material, and he controls his own imaginative response to it with patient care. It is only toward the end of the novel that we realize for sure the immensity of Henchard's pain and the intensity of his tragedy, and we can accept it there, because of the narrative and dramatic preparation Hardy has made earlier. He has constructed a world which expands in time, metaphorically, to accommodate first Henchard's specific past and then Henchard himself, as representative man. His fate is made slowly, cumulatively, though it is foreshadowed from the very beginning. Ironies accumulate, as events recur one after another from the past to buffet Henchard for his mistake. At each turn he is defeated, but he never surrenders. He blots out his dignity, but each time he returns to the struggle with a new determination. We are sure, finally, of his stature and its legitimacy as we see his resolution in the face of his fate, as that fate is fulfilled. He has left Elizabeth-Jane, knowing the physical return of Sailor Newson to be imminent, and he walks out on the road across the heath:

> He went on till he came to the first milestone, which stood in the bank, half way up a steep hill. He rested his basket on the top of the stone, placed his elbows on it, and gave way to a convulsive twitch, which was worse than a sob, because it was so hard and dry.
>
> "If I had only got her with me—If I only had! Hard work would mean nothing to me then! But that was not to be. I—Cain—go alone as I deserve—an outcast and a vagabond. But my punishment is *not* greater than I can bear!"

This is Henchard, trying for once to articulate his pain, trying to express his determination against despair. In the awkward, stumbling lines that he utters his tragedy becomes obvious; with the whole action of the novel behind them, these stilted and stifled words of Henchard's describe in him the strength of man's soul. And as Cain, the firstborn son of Adam, he achieves that awful dignity which characterizes tragic —and heroic—man.

The novel opens as Henchard, Susan, and Elizabeth-Jane approach Weydon Priors. For six paragraphs not a word is spoken as character and adumbrations of the fate of man, setting and the metaphoric extension of setting in time are described. Henchard is a young man of twenty, a haytrusser, taciturn and phlegmatic in his attitude. (The detail of his walk given here will be repeated in amended form as he leaves Casterbridge almost twenty-five years later, and walks to that milestone on the heath.) Susan is represented as having "the hard, half-apathetic expression of one who deems anything possible at the hands of Time and Chance, except, perhaps, fair play." And though there are two bad editorial intrusions—almost a rarity in this novel—immediately after the lines quoted, these lines are legitimately descriptive of Susan's attitude. What this pantomine or moving tableau shows us of Henchard and Susan is so precise in its meaning that we can readily accept such a generalization about her character.

Hardy insists on a close and minute awareness of physical objects, of motions, of sounds; it is from this attention to details that he forms his vision as a novelist and as a poet. And from this kind of scrutiny he suggests the intensity of existence which, without such attention, would be missed. Just before Michael and Susan meet a man from Weydon Priors and begin to speak with him—just, that is, at the end of this opening dumb show—Hardy introduces the sound of a pathetic bird-song in the background, and suggests through this the unchanging and timeless fate of man:

> For a long time there was none [i.e., no sound], beyond the voice of a weak bird singing a trite old evening song that might doubtless have been heard on the hill at the same hour, and with the self-same trills, quavers, and breves, at any sunset of that season for centuries untold.

The fair at Weydon Priors is introduced through the turnip-hoer they meet, and Henchard and his family proceed there, to the introduction of the furmity-woman, a "haggish creature of about fifty" who provides for Henchard's downfall with her rum. She is the carrier, in a sense, of the guilt of the novel: of Michael Henchard's guilt, in which she has such a large part, as trafficker in illegitimate and evil things. She is set here as the embassy of evil, the character opposed to Susan and to whom Henchard is attracted. The furmity-woman appears four times in the novel: here, as witness and accessory to Henchard's mistake; in chapter 3, when Susan returns to Weydon fair-field to find the way to Henchard's present; in chapter 28, to expose Henchard's past at Weydon Priors in his present; and finally in chapter 36, to urge one more discovering of the past, this time of Henchard's past with Lucetta. The furmity-woman gives Henchard drink, and he proposes the sale of his wife: "She shall take the girl if she wants to, and go her ways. I'll take my tools, and go my ways. 'Tis simple as Scripture history." The simplicity which characterizes Henchard's speech here stands for the blocked, seemingly spare lines of the whole novel; and such terrible compressed simplicity actually does suggest "Scripture history." This is Henchard, blindly describing his own future, in which he becomes a Cain who begs not to be removed from existence but to be removed from memory: to have his existence forgotten, because of the burden of his past.

But what seems to be biblical spareness and straightness, and what seems to be Henchard's simple and straight fate, cannot be so; time is already set up with a complexity that denies the possibility of a simple present. It is the past that will occur in the dramatic and ironic unfolding of chronology. As Susan, sold by her husband for five guineas, leaves the furmity-tent with Sailor Newson, one of the women cries out, "I'd go, and 'a might call, and call, till his keacorn was raw; but I'd never come back—no, not till the great trumpet, would I!" This

"Scripture history" of Michael Henchard's life expands, eventually, through such suggestions as this, so that his "moment" of existence in the long history of the world begins "at the beginning," at "the Creation"—as he commits his sin of wife-selling at Weydon fair-field—and ends only when things have come full circle, when his past has been fulfilled as his present or future, when the Apocalyptic days of Revelations are lived out and the "great trumpet" mentioned in this opening chapter has sounded him out of existence. Through its artistically planned recurrence in various ways throughout the novel, this opening scene at Weydon Priors becomes the emblem of the fatal transcendence of time in *The Mayor of Casterbridge*. This transcendence is not simply the return of the past or the central character's past, however; Hardy uses his setting metaphorically, bringing all of history and prehistory into the present existence of the novel, to emphasize actual recurrence and to justify such, symbolically, as natural phenomena in a dramatically intense world. As the intensity of the physical situation and its largeness in time are being established, the hero's simple story attaches simultaneously to this larger scheme so that he becomes, through the narrative presentation of his tragedy on this stage, a man representative of all men in all of time. The immensity of this symbolic identity is compressed for Henchard into a single moment of existence which is as timeless as eternity. As his existence transcends time it transcends individual existence, and he assumes the size and spiritual stature Hardy has set out to give him as "a Man of Character."

Beach says that "Hardy's greatness lies...in the association of events with the setting in which they occur" (*The Twentieth Century Novel*). Earlier he makes a more perceptive comment about Hardy and his use of setting. He speaks of Hardy's "time-vision which is one of the richest resources of the poet" as this is used in depicting character. This vision he describes as the "faculty of setting the plainest figures of today in a perspective of ages, in a shadowy synthesis that, while it dwarfs the present scene, yet lends it a grandeur, too, a dignity and a noble pathos borrowed from those of time itself." Harold Child reaches a similar conclusion in trying to explain Hardy's use of history and historical references: "The insignificance of man, the briefness of his days, are always present in Hardy's mind; he never fails to see them from the point of view of the indifferent power, and the enormous past is always with him as a moment of time." The emphasis on man's "insignificance" is an oversimplification which distorts Hardy's artistic as well as his philosophical vision; but the awareness of the influence of time and historical setting in time expressed by both Beach and Child is significant.

Julian Moynahan, in an article on *The Mayor of Casterbridge,* finds in it a "remarkable sense of continuity of the past with present times which is expressed through the archaeological features of the setting." And J. H. Fowler, after quoting some lines from the opening chapters of *The Return of the Native,* says of Hardy's use of time and history for plot and setting:

> Nothing is more characteristic of Hardy than the deep sense, to which these passages bear eloquent testimony, of the antiquity of man and the still greater antiquity of the earth. "The thing that hath been is the thing that shall be, and there is no new thing under the sun." That sentiment is as old as Ecclesiastes, but the feeling expressed by Hardy is more complex and is the direct result of modern discoveries. Ecclesiastes, in other words, merely thinks of human existence as the purposeless repetition of the same monotonous acts. Hardy's thought is rather of the continuity of existence —each act that we do, each sight that we look on, reaching back into an incredibly remote past, with no break in the links that bind us to the beginning of time.

Representing the continuity of man's existence in the long history of the world, however, is not in itself worth much. And if the grandeur of the universe is set up to diminish man, then the artist loses his hero. Although at times Hardy does stress the comparative finitude of man's stature, his technique is most essentially directed toward the exaggeration of man's size, and he describes this heroic size for man through the metaphoric reference of time and history. Man's life—at any rate, Michael Henchard's life—is so short in terms of universal or cosmic history that his existence becomes momentary and, through the intensity of that moment, so long as to measure in its experience all of time.

Late in *The Mayor of Casterbridge,* after Henchard's past has been exposed by the furmity-woman, Sailor Newson returns to Casterbridge. Henchard's discovery of this (a preview, since Newson on this occasion does not actually come into the town) is one of the dramatic climaxes of the novel. The setting is given, linking the time of the scene in the chronology of the novel to prehistory:

> Two miles out, a quarter of a mile from the highway, was the prehistoric fort called Mai Dun, of huge dimensions and

many ramparts, within or upon whose enclosures a human being, as seen from the road, was but an insignificant speck. Hitherward Henchard often resorted, glass in hand, and scanned the hedgeless *Via*—for it was the original track laid out by the legions of the Empire.

The stage for the action is thus built, and our attention is attracted to it and to the relatively small figure occupying it. I would say about this stage what Guerard says about Maumbury Ring, as he remembers it from a schoolboy reading: that the grand image of "Hadrian's soldiery mysteriously reappearing in broad daylight" is called up "in one rather pedestrian sentence." Guerard continues:

> The point I want to make is simple enough. Not subtlety or elaboration of art but the imagined material itself gives the best scenes of the novel their strength. And Hardy had the instinct or the art to let this material speak for itself. He becomes diffuse or flabbily abstract only when the material is inadequate, or when he is not himself convinced of its truth.

The scene at the Ring is carefully set, so that Hadrian's soldiers may come quickly alive at the moment of their mention. Similarly, the scene at Mai Dun is set, not with "subtlety or elaboration of art," but through reference to the effect already achieved in "the imagined material itself," through the introduction of another of those ancient and time-transcending places which provide the basic supportive mood of the whole novel.

Once the stage is ready, and Henchard is placed upon it, Hardy creates what amounts to an immediate vacuum in time, a briefly spotted eternity for the action of the scene. Henchard happens to be on this spot, happens to look with his telescope in the right direction, and sees on the horizon the sailor who bought his wife twenty years ago. Henchard's past is imposed on his present, on the authority of the metaphoric juxtaposition of prehistory and the present in the setting. Henchard, paralyzed on the spot by the recognition of Newson's face, "lived a lifetime the moment he saw it."

For the important scenes of the novel, Hardy forces chronological time out and replaces it with the still, simple, static and intense moments of timelessness. What is achieved is the creation of something like tragic "spots of time." Around and on scenes so spotted Hardy builds *The Mayor of Casterbridge*. The scenes are almost invariably coincidental, in the large sense of the term: each scene is the dramatization of a fatal juxtaposition of events, and the intensity of the lives involved makes the grotesque juxtaposition legitimate.

The Mai Dun scene is a good example of what can be proposed as Hardy's awareness of the effect he was creating through the use of this technique. In the manuscript of *The Mayor of Casterbridge* its original casting is very different, and its effect is much less.

At the close of chapter 42 Henchard eavesdrops on Elizabeth-Jane and Farfrae and discovers the seriousness of their courtship. In the manuscript, Henchard first listens from his hiding place as Farfrae calls her "Dear Elizabeth-Jane" (fol. 442). He knows where they often meet, and in the next paragraph he goes out along the Budmouth road to observe them:

> The absorbing interest which the courtship—as it evidently now was—had for Henchard, led him to a further step. A quarter of a mile from the highway was a prehistoric earthen fort of huge dimensions and many ramparts, within or upon whose enclosure a human being, as seen from the road, was but an insignificant speck. Hither Henchard resorted, glass in hand, and scanned the hedgeless *Via*—for it was the original track laid out by the legions of the Empire—to a distance of two or three miles. His step-daughter had passed by on her walk some time before; and she presently emerged from a cutting in the hill, bound homeward.
>
> Then a figure came from behind the Ring at the other edge of the landscape, and advanced to meet her half-way. Applying his spyglass, Farfrae was discovered. They met, joined hands, and—Donald kissed her, Elizabeth-Jane looking quickly round to assure herself that nobody was near.
>
> (Fols. 442–43)

There are numerous things wrong with these paragraphs. The introduction of Mai Dun and the mention of the Ring are purposeless, since they are not used. Mai Dun is wasted under Henchard because the scene doesn't measure up to what the setting suggests. The Ring, set with its long and still vital past, means nothing for Farfrae or Elizabeth-Jane, so it is useless to have Farfrae emerge from behind its slopes. The telescope is not symbolic but an appendage, as it is used neither to contract distance nor to focus. Rather, it is used awkwardly to pan from one side to the other, swinging from Elizabeth-Jane walking up from the south to Farfrae walking out from the north. And Elizabeth-Jane, one is told, is coming from one of her meetings with Newson, whom she is supposed to see "two or three times a week" (fols. 450–51).

In the revision of this scene, Elizabeth-Jane's walks are innocent if coy exercises in meeting Farfrae; she does not know anything about Newson. When Henchard goes out onto Mai Dun "to read the progress of affairs between Farfrae and his charmer," he already knows that Farfrae calls her "Dearest Elizabeth-Jane" and that he has kissed her, since these two minor discoveries are pulled together into the one brief scene which Henchard observes from hiding in the Ring. What happens—what Henchard sees—in the revision of the Mai Dun scene, however, is of major importance. Henchard puts his telescope to his eye as he stands on the outer ring of the prehistoric fort, looking to find Elizabeth-Jane and Farfrae meeting again. Elizabeth-Jane represents his past, standing for the daughter he sold. As he scans the old Roman road through his glass, he sees the man from that past walking into his present. The telescope now serves as a useful symbol: it reminds the reader that space, events, and time can be compressed, and that the distant can be brought close. The useless reference to the Ring has been eliminated, the distraction of looking all up and down the landscape is removed, and only Henchard, Newson, the telescope, and Mai Dun are left. There was no significance to the historical aspect of the castle when Henchard used it as a stage from which to observe Elizabeth-Jane and Farfrae kissing. But now it serves to set up the intrusion of the past, and the irony of Henchard's standing upon the ruins of a prehistoric past still extant in the present is inherent in the scene: the Michael Henchard of 1850 calls up his own past from 1830, through the symbolic agency of a telescope.

The change in the meaning of the scene is immense. From this scene, as revised, comes the climax of the novel. Newson appears, his face is recognized, and time stops: "Henchard lived a lifetime the moment he saw it." He can't move, and in the violence of this timeless, motionless situation, Henchard's whole life is spent. His past has imposed itself finally, physically, upon his present: and his future, too, is spent. When he is dead, his last will is read: "& that no man remember me." The tormented soul, on its way to eternal timelessness, asks to have this timeless, intense moment which has been its human existence isolated from the more normal and less tragic history of man.

Maumbury Ring is Hardy's other important symbolic stage in *The Mayor of Casterbridge,* and its very richly detailed representation sets much of the emphasis for the later descriptions of Mai Dun, several minor stages, and, at the end, Egdon Heath. The Ring is, for Hardy, "merely the local name of one of the finest Roman Amphitheatres, if not the very finest, remaining in Britain." It occupies a prominent spot at the edge of Casterbridge, which

> announced old Rome in every street, alley, and precinct. It looked Roman, bespoke the art of Rome, concealed dead men of Rome. It was impossible to dig more than a foot or two deep about the town fields and gardens without coming upon some tall soldier or other of the Empire, who had lain there in his silent unobtrusive rest for a space of fifteen hundred years.

This historical aspect of the setting, however, seems remote from Michael Henchard's drama, and little more than a dead past which has buried its dead: "They had lived so long ago, their time was so unlike the present, their hopes and motives were so widely removed from ours, that between them and the living there seemed to stretch a gulf too wide for even a spirit to pass."

But despite the fact of time, despite the remoteness of the Roman past, which he admits, Hardy insists on mood and impression: the Ring is to ancient-rooted Casterbridge "what the ruined Coliseum is to modern Rome," and "the dusk of evening . . . the proper hour at which a true impression of this suggestive place could be received." According to this "impression," the arena is "still smooth and circular, as if used for its original purpose not so very long ago." It is mysteriously "suggestive" too, and has established itself in local tradition:

> for some old people said that at certain moments in the summer time, in broad daylight, persons sitting with a book or dozing in the arena had, on lifting their eyes beheld the slopes lined with a gazing legion of Hadrian's soldiery as if watching the gladiatorial combat; and had heard the roar of their excited voices; that the scene would last but a moment, like a lightning flash, and then disappear.

The result of this description, the best and most elaborate metaphoric use of setting in all of Hardy's works, is the firm establishment of a past still existing, still living in the present. This is the spot Henchard chooses, then "as being the safest from observation which he could think of for meeting his long-lost wife." Their meeting, "in the middle of the arena," is parallel to and even suggested by the recurrence of

Rome and Romans: for Susan brings the past, alive, into the present. The thematic result of their meeting, of course, is their decision to remarry: again, to bring an event out of the past to its conscious, ritualistic re-creation and reenactment in the present.

Susan is known, ironically, as "the Ghost" to the boys of Casterbridge—as the ghost from the past, haunting the present into which she has come to make her claim. When she dies, she is buried with a past more antique than hers, in

> the still-used burial ground of the old Roman–British city, whose curious feature was this, its continuity as a place of sepulture. Mrs. Henchard's dust mingled with the dust of women who lay ornamented with glass hairpins and amber necklaces, and men who held in their mouths coins of Hadrian, Posthumus, and the Constantines.

It is perhaps awkward and hard to accept Susan's consorting, even in death, with historical figures. But we are reminded of her arrival in Casterbridge and that first meeting with Henchard by the historical reference of this scene. And the spot is used immediately to begin another stylized part of the novel, with the introduction of Lucetta. Evidently Hardy originally did not plan to juxtapose Elizabeth-Jane's visit to Susan's grave with the introduction of Lucetta. The narrative section quoted above does not appear in the manuscript at all, and when she meets Lucetta, Elizabeth-Jane is said to be out for a walk in the woods rather than on a visit to her mother's grave. But in the first conceived scene, Hardy was working in a similar direction, and Elizabeth-Jane was already thinking of Romans and the Ring and Mai Dun:

> So Elizabeth-Jane walked and read, or looked about and thought of the shadowy beings she mentally designated as "Romans" who had laid out these square angles and banks, and that earthen theatre hard by, and that stupendous fort which rose against the sky behind.
>
> (Fols. 193–94)

Still, it is of no significance that Elizabeth-Jane thinks of Romans, or notices ancient earthworks. But if Hardy makes the association more specific, as he does in the revision for the published text of the novel, he can make a dramatic connection through the historical reference, and thus make the coincidence of the meeting of Elizabeth-Jane and Lucetta aesthetically acceptable, through the effect of the metaphorical setting. Two people whose meeting will be seen as appropriate as soon as it occurs, meet in a place which will reinforce that appropriateness. Elizabeth-Jane visits her mother's grave, and the description of this spot reminds one of the Ring, where Susan met Michael when she first arose out of his dead past into his present. Also visiting Susan's grave in this "churchyard old as civilization" is Lucetta, another figure out of Henchard's past.

Lucetta's function in the novel will have to be discussed again later in this chapter. I might point out here, however, that she is associated with Henchard's past, and has a past herself, and like Henchard is destroyed by her past, by that part she shared illegitimately with him. Still, Lucetta is only a small type, at best, of Henchard. She determines to be free, saying, "I won't be a slave to the past—I'll love where I choose!" —and upon Henchard's exposure she runs away to marry Farfrae.

The stage which was set for Susan and Henchard to meet on is used by Lucetta and Henchard and seems ready to accept Lucetta and Farfrae. In the manuscript Hardy's temporary, perhaps momentary intention was to have them meet there:

> During the day she went out to the Ring, and by chance or design a figure met her there. As soon as she saw Elizabeth-Jane after her return indoors she told her she had decided to go away from home to the seaside—to Port Bredy for a few days. Casterbridge was so gloomy.
>
> (Fol. 289)

But the opening lines of the paragraph are cancelled, and the sentence is revised to read, "During the day she went out to the Ring, and to other places, not coming in till nearly dusk." It seems as though Hardy's original intention was to have Farfrae and Lucetta meet and decide to marry at the same spot that Henchard chose for his first meeting with Susan and his sort of second Susan, Lucetta. Since the sentence is made ambiguous now, and since they do in fact marry at Port Bredy within the next three days, perhaps they still do meet at the Ring: whatever the case may be, Hardy has removed the emphasis on what would have been an irrelevant coincidence, and the reference to the Ring is now just a passing allusion to a prominent landmark in the city. For the metaphoric unity of the novel it is hardly legitimate for Farfrae, the outsider who has no past at all, to use the Ring to meet Lucetta, whose only past is with Henchard on the Isle of Jersey. The Ring, like Mai Dun, is reserved for more purposeful symbolic uses than this.

If this restriction on the use of the Ring eliminates one of the parallels of the novel, it does not change the effect of the extreme stylization of the entire work. In some sense, only one thing happens in the novel: Michael Henchard sells his wife. As he awakes the morning after this he wonders, "Did I tell my name to anybody last night, or didn't I tell my name?" and, at the end of the novel, when his guilt has grown from name through soul, he asks "that no man remember me." The wife-selling recurs in reminders throughout the story: both Henchard and the reader are kept continually aware of it. When Susan returns to Weydon Priors in chapter 3 to try to find Michael, she asks the furmity-woman, "Can you call to mind...the sale of a wife by her husband in your tent eighteen years ago today?" and chapter 4 begins with a reference to that "tragical crisis...the transaction at Weydon Fair." Henchard is described in Casterbridge, in chapter 17, as being made of "the same unruly volcanic stuff...as when he had sold his wife at Weydon Fair." And Michael, begging Elizabeth-Jane to accept him as her father after Susan's death, reminds himself of his past crime as he says to her, "Don't take against me—though I was a drunken man once, and used your mother roughly—I'll be kinder to you than *he* was."

Not only do these allusions keep us aware of what specific mistake committed at what specific time and place is Henchard's tragic fault, his *hamartia;* they also insist that that past is not dead, that it still exists in the present. Susan brings it in herself; Henchard is still made of the same stuff now as then; and his confession of what he once was, which he wants to atone for now, is the expression of his own conviction first that that past is still vital and can be reworked and remolded in his present, and second that whatever punishment or pain comes to him now is but "what he had deserved."

From the beginning Henchard recognizes his fault in selling Susan, and his responsibility for his act. When he awakens from his drunkenness the morning after he has sold her, he reflects that his grief, his guilt "was of his own making, and he ought to bear it." He wants to believe that he can make "a start in a new direction" after this. But "Character is Fate" in Hardy's world of causal relationships, and twenty years after this act and his attempt at reform, Henchard will feel again that pain is "what he had deserved." His only triumph is in the heroic determination which closes his career, as he accepts this fate, finally and irrevocably, in his loneliness: "I—Cain—go alone as I deserve—an outcast and a vagabond. But my punishment is *not* greater than I can bear."

The recurrence of Weydon Priors as one of the important places of the novel also reminds us of what happened there. Susan, sold and gone from there, must return there with Elizabeth-Jane to find her way back to Henchard. And Henchard himself finally returns there, too, in chapter 44. The first two visits are set up very carefully as parallels, and part of the effect of this is to bridge the gap of nearly twenty years between chapter 2 and chapter 3. The last visit is set up as a dramatic, symbolic, almost ritualistic repetition of that first trip, too, only this time Henchard is alone. He has been walking away from Casterbridge for five days. "It now became apparent that the direction of his journey was Weydon Priors, which he reached on the afternoon of the sixth day." His pilgrimage is a return to the beginning of it all: he is returning to the scene of the crime. Symbolically, he is turning things full circle, preparing for the end.

Henchard is from the beginning a man of forms and symbols. In preparing to swear his oath "to avoid all strong liquors for the space of twenty years" he requires "a fit place and imagery; for there was something fetichistic in this man's beliefs." He requires the choir at the Three Mariners—who are sitting by "like the monolithic circle at Stonehenge in its pristine days"—to sing a formal curse for Donald Farfrae. He insists on the form of his previous dignity as mayor, wearing "the fretted and weather-beaten garments of bygone years," "the very clothes which he had used to wear in the primal days" of his mayoralty, and he meets the Royal personage this way, waving a flag in his hand. Finally, in writing his last will and tacking it above his head he makes his last gesture toward ordering and dignifying his existence—which is what all form and ritual are for.

Perhaps because of Henchard's ritualistic awareness, his "fetichistic" psychological makeup, the suggestiveness of the repetitions through-out the novel is never lost on him. As he makes the choir at the tavern sing the psalm to curse Farfrae, he explains his irony to them: "As for him, it was partly by his songs that he got me over, and heaved me out." Later, as Henchard sits in the loft of the granary waiting to challenge Farfrae to physical combat, Farfrae unwittingly turns the irony back on him, by humming

> a song he had sung when he arrived years before at the Three Mariners, a poor young man, adventuring for life and fortune, and scarcely knowing whitherwards:—
> "And here's a hand, my trusty fiere,
> And gie's a hand o' thine."

Nothing moved Henchard like an old melody. He sank back. "No; I can't do it!" he gasped.

Finally, in his last will, Henchard unravels all his mistakes, and untwists the curse he had sung for Farfrae to apply it to himself. Those verses from the psalm, "And the next age his hated name / Shall utterly deface," are repeated in Michael's final and summary request, "that no man remember me."

There are other examples of repetition, which need not be explicated in depth here. Henchard's dependence on the weather twice ruins him: in chapter 16, when his planned holiday entertainments at Poundbury Ring are ruined by rain, and he loses face to Farfrae; and in chapter 27, at the harvest, when it is "more like living in Revelations . . . than in England," when the end of the world does come, financially, for Henchard, as he misguesses the weather. And there are striking parallels as well as serious artistic achievements in the death scenes of Susan, in chapter 18, and Lucetta, in chapter 40.

Lucetta's whole existence in the novel is interesting in its formal artistic conception. She is a continuation of Susan, a second character coming up out of Henchard's past. At the same time, however, she is a partial Gloucester to Henchard's Lear, running through the same or similar griefs with him, suffering for and destroyed by the past she shares with him. She tries to break from the bonds of her past, and this destroys her. The past cannot be forgotten because it cannot be made to die. Henchard reads her old love letters to himself aloud for her husband, Farfrae, and "her own words greeted her in Henchard's voice, like spirits from the grave." In reading the letters, Henchard is tempting himself to what he thinks will destroy Farfrae—the exposure of the past. But Farfrae's happiness and success are tied best to the future, only momentarily to the present, and not at all to the past. The letters represent Lucetta's past, and her happiness is dependent on keeping that past hidden. When it is exposed—economically, through the agency of Henchard's own destroyers, the furmity-woman and Jopp —Lucetta is destroyed. The town revives an old custom, and has a skimmity-ride, depicting Lucetta's past with Henchard. The shock is so great for her that she has a miscarriage, thus losing the future she has planned with Farfrae, and dies.

Henchard's fault in relation to Lucetta is similar to his fault in relation to Susan, so that Lucetta's role in the novel becomes in part a reworking of Susan's to heighten the effect. Repetition and the suggestion of repetition through the stylization of material represent the intensity of existence that Hardy wants. This intensity is suggested by the structure of the novel; it is supported, metaphorically, by the setting and by numerous descriptive and dramatic references; and it is actual in the real, literal, and specific juxtaposition of past and present, in the intrusion of certain past events into the present. This intrusion is dramatized as coincidence, and its dramatic effect—the past repeating itself, displacing the present—is the creation of that timelessness which allows the expansion of character and incident to a universal significance.

The two major stages in *The Mayor of Casterbridge* have been examined at some length. The whole of Casterbridge is a "stage," and there are several other, smaller ones which are constructed on principles at least similar to those employed in the construction of the Ring and Mai Dun. High Place Hall, the house Lucetta takes in Casterbridge, represents metaphorically the past and the unhappy reconstruction of it, at the same time that it stands as a sort of gray *memento mori,* representative of the humility of human accomplishments. Ten Hatches Hole, where Henchard goes to commit suicide, is described briefly as "a circular pool formed by the wash of centuries." This seemingly insignificant detail, despite its brevity, operates in the metaphoric context of the whole novel. It is at Ten Hatches Hole that Henchard prepares to take his life, but he is saved by the most grotesque of coincidences: he sees himself floating in the water beneath him. The ironic and exactly timed intrusion of the effigy from the skimmity-ride becomes all the more a dramatic, symbolic interference if one accepts that Ten Hatches Hole exists in an expanded time that runs for "centuries." As both irony and coincidence grow larger, they make Henchard more important, so that it is not just his own life he contemplates taking, but that of the hero in us all. Smaller lives—Lucetta's, the effigy's—have been sacrificed to save him, because, Hardy insists, Henchard is worth more and can bear more.

The last stage Hardy describes is his general Wessex stage, Egdon Heath. Egdon is the world—or like it—and Henchard walks out into it to die. It is "that ancient country whose surface never had been stirred to a finger's depth, save by the scratching of rabbits, since brushed by the feet of the earliest tribes." And if all Michael Henchard has done in the face of his fate is scratch at the surface of this timeless immensity, still he has risen as man in the dignity of his effort, and his scratching is etched along with the brushing of the feet of those earliest tribes on the history of man and his world.

There are a number of statements of compression or expansion of time in *The Mayor of Casterbridge.* Dealer Buzzford casually introduces this technique in the remark which serves as the epigraph for this chapter: "Casterbridge is a old, hoary place o' wickedness, by all account. 'Tis recorded in history that we rebelled against the King one or two hundred years ago, in the time of the Romans." Hardy worked carefully with this humorous and cleverly effective bit of historical inaccuracy. The original form the statement takes in the manuscript is straight, simple, and accurate:

> hoary
> "Casterbridge is a old ~~ancient~~ place o'wickedness, by all
> rebelled against
> account. 'Tis recorded in history that we ~~helped kill~~ the King
> one or
> ~~about~~ two hundred years ago; and for my part, I can well
> believe it."
>
> (Fol. 73)

Then, by means of an interlinear addition, Hardy pushes the "one or two hundred years ago" past back into "the time of the Romans," and all of history is foreshortened.

Something similar happens in the furmity-woman's scene at court. She is described, first, as

> an old woman of mottled countenance, attired in a shawl of that nameless tertiary hue which comes, but cannot be made —a hue neither tawny, russet, hazel, nor ash; a sticky black bonnet that seemed to have been worn in the country of the Psalmist where the clouds drop fatness; and in an apron that had been white in times so comparatively recent as to contrast visibly with the rest of her clothes. The steeped aspect of the woman as a whole showed her to be no native of the country-side or even of a country-town.

This description seems deliberately calculated to elude time. The furmity-woman is said to belong to no local place, though we know her only from Weydon Priors to Casterbridge. When she first appeared in the novel, in its opening chapter, her apron was white—and now the time of that whiteness, twenty years ago, is suggested as "comparatively recent" in her history, and is pushed thus into proximity with the present. Then she begins to tell the story of that earlier time:

> "Twenty years ago or thereabout I was a selling of furmity in a tent at Weydon Fair—"
> " 'Twenty years ago'—well, that's beginning at the beginning; suppose you go back to the Creation!" said the clerk, not without satire.
> But Henchard stared, and quite forgot what was evidence and what was not.

The end is the same as that of the other example given, to make the present representatively larger. The technique, however, is slightly different. The past—of twenty years and of all of time—is condensed so that the present can encompass more of it, and the scene in the present is expanded and taken back through time to cover all the past. To effect this expansion, Hardy again revised carefully. The descriptive paragraph quoted above is written into the manuscript in almost final form. But the dialogue that follows has one important interlinear addition, which seems to be evidence of Hardy's awareness of what he was doing. After the clerk says, "well, that's beginning at the beginning," Hardy inserts a new line for him, "suppose you go back to the Creation!" (fol. 287), which emphasizes the ironically suggested expansion.

A third quotable example of the seemingly deliberate creation of metaphors of timelessness through dialogue occurs in chapter 26, as Henchard goes to see Mr. Fall, the weather-prophet. Henchard asks him how he is sure of his prediction of "tempest" for the harvest time.

> "You are not certain, of course?"
> "As one can be in a world where all's unsure. 'Twill be more like living in Revelations this autumn than in England. Shall I sketch it out for 'ee in a scheme?"

This adumbration of Henchard's fall is done in apocalyptic terms, and through the suggestion of a larger world and a universal time for him to act in, his destruction becomes, symbolically, the end of the world. Again, Hardy works out the line in the manuscript. The first legible draft seems to make no sense at all: "'Twill be as much like living in Revelations this autumn as living elsewhere can be" (fol. 268). The main idea is already there, perhaps having somehow suggested itself. But the term and the idea have yet to be turned from expletive reference to thematic and dramatic metaphor, which is what Hardy does, finally. The manuscript looks like this:

```
                  more
"'Twill be as much [?] like living in Revelations this autumn
        than              in England
      as living elsewhere can be."
```

This kind of atmosphere legitimizes the action of *The Mayor of Casterbridge.* After the exposure of Henchard's Weydon Priors past in the present of Casterbridge, Hardy explains its importance in terms of this atmosphere:

> Had the incident been well known of old and always, it might by this time have grown to be lightly regarded as the rather tall wild oat. . .of a young man, with whom the steady and mature (if somewhat headstrong) burgher of today had scarcely a point in common. But the act having lain as dead and buried ever since, the interspace of years was unperceived; and the black spot of his youth wore the aspect of a recent crime.

It is because of the characteristic mood of the novel, too, that Newson can pop in and out, dramatically, as he does. And though this mood would suggest that his entrance needs little preparation, still Hardy sets each appearance he makes. The first time he visits Henchard, the corn-factor is living in Jopp's house, which is set with the casual apostrophe of "trees which seemed old enough to have been planted by the friars" of the old Franciscan Priory, in ruins close by. "The cottage itself," the narrator continues, "was built of old stones from the long dismantled Priory," and stands near the spot of the original mill where the water has "raised its roar for centuries."

This setting detail, small as it may seem, still serves to maintain the mood of the novel, and thus helps to justify the coincidence of Newson's return. In presenting Newson's return, Hardy chooses, as he often does, to emphasize the coincidence. Newson has stopped by once, while Henchard is out attending the death of Lucetta. When he returns, Jopp describes the visitor, who "gave no name, and no message." Henchard replies to this, "Nor do I gi'e him any attention." Newson returns in the next chapter, and confronts Henchard: "So here I am. Now—that transaction between us some twenty years agone—'tis that I've called about." The intrusion is so sudden—and then, equally quickly, it is over, and he is gone. Henchard tells him that both Susan and Elizabeth-Jane are dead, and he departs: "Henchard heard the retreating footsteps upon the sanded floor, the mechanical lifting of the latch. . .

Newson's shadow passed the window. He was gone." Henchard's lie "had been the impulse of a moment"—and the next time Newson returns, Henchard lives his whole "lifetime" in that "moment."

One of the major objections to *The Mayor of Casterbridge* is Albert Guerard's complaint that the novel is too long, that chapters 28–30 and 36–40 are grossly overplotted. The chapters he cites are, for the most part, weak, though the finely done court scene of chapter 28 is essential, and the end of chapter 40 contains those few, beautiful lines that make up the representation of Lucetta's death. But Guerard appreciates the power of *The Mayor of Casterbridge,* and it seems to be this appreciation that makes him call attention to what he sees as its flaws. (One wonders if he means to include chapter 28 in his blacklist, since he says that the furmity-woman's return is unforgettable for him, and central to that stylized formality which makes the novel.) Similarly, I am tempted to call attention to the instances of editorial interference in the novel, simply because they are so few. Hardy rarely—never, in the rest of his fiction—had or exercised the patience and control which is so obvious in his handling of *The Mayor of Casterbridge. Tess of the D'Urbervilles,* perhaps the next best of his novels, is marred by his editorializing and by his frequent perversion of the narrative character and point of view. He solves the problem in part in this novel by his conception of Elizabeth-Jane. She views the world much as Tess does; but she is not the central character, and she is set up to assume, logically and reasonably, the point of view assigned her. Elizabeth-Jane inherits from her mother—"one who deems anything possible at the hands of Time or Chance except, perhaps, fair play"—her vision of life. She sees early that life is "a tragical rather than a comical thing; that though one could be gay on occasion, moments of gaiety were interludes, and no part of the actual drama." As Elizabeth-Jane develops (too quickly, in chapters 24 and 25) the narrator rephrases her philosophy for her:

> Yet her experience had consisted less of pure disappointments than in a series of substitutions. Continually it had happened that what she had desired had not been granted her, and that what had been granted her she had not desired.

Finally, in the conclusion of the novel, we are told for the last time what Elizabeth-Jane's vision is, and it is effectively Hardy's own vision, justified by the "experience" of the novel. Elizabeth-Jane serves as interpreter of the experience of Henchard's intense and tragic existence for the normal world. Her awareness keeps the novel in the world of actual people and actual England in a specific mid-nineteenth-century time.

The story Elizabeth-Jane interprets is the story of "Faust"—who sold something of his, too, for some twenty-odd years of happiness; of a Job-like creature, for a moment; of "Cain," our brother. Henchard has been the "great tree in a wind," "a vehement gloomy being," "a dark ruin" in the course of the novel. And in the end he is the great silent creature who faces his fate and is overcome.

I said at the beginning of this study of Hardy's technique [The Metaphor of Chance] that one of the curious things about his art was his inability to make his characters speak. This generalization has been qualified several times for the minor novels. However, in The Mayor of Casterbridge it is too exactly true, and still the novel is a great dramatic success. Characters don't talk things out; they stand mutely facing each other while the narrator explains. Elizabeth-Jane doesn't tell anyone how she feels about life; rather, the narrator explains her vision to the reader. And Henchard's last will is not only written rather than spoken, it is delivered to Elizabeth-Jane by an intermediate character who cannot even read. Perhaps this device—or trick—is really very effective for the dramatization of Henchard's character, for since Whittle can't read, the original power of the statement is saved for the moment of its disclosure, though Henchard himself has been dead for half an hour.

Henchard's silence is total: his only speech is that grand, turgid, wrenched Cain speech. Silence finally pervades his whole existence—past, present, and the future that never comes to be. His will is:

> "That Elizabeth-Jane Farfrae not to be told of my death,
>   or made to grieve on account of me.
>   "& that I be not bury'd in consecrated ground.
>   "& that no sexton be asked to toll the bell.
>   "& that nobody is wished to see my dead body.
>   "& that no murners walk behind me at my funeral.
>   "& that no flours be planted on my grave.
>   "& that no man remember me.
>   "To this I put my name.
>   "Michael Henchard."

In the chapter of Sartor Resartus entitled "Symbols," Teufelsdrockh says, "Speech is of Time, Silence is of Eternity." And in response to Henchard's last silence, Elizabeth-Jane says, "But, there's no altering—

so it must be." An intensified, imperative "Amen" is all one can say to the career, the fate, the will of Michael Henchard: "so it must be."

Then the world is relaxed, diminished, and returned to its more usual self and size. As this happens, Hardy reiterates Elizabeth-Jane's vision, her understanding through experience—as a reminder, perhaps, of that intense repetition which has been the core of the novel: "Her experience had been of a kind to teach her, rightly or wrongly, that the doubtful honor of a brief transit through a sorry world hardly called for effusiveness." But she is now fortunate, and a new horizon has appeared for her. Still, Henchard's tragedy has been an experience, a lesson in life, not just a catharsis. And as the novel concludes,

> she did not cease to wonder at the persistence of the unforeseen, when the one to whom such unbroken tranquility had been accorded in the adult stage was she whose youth had seemed to teach that happiness was but the occasional episode in a general drama of pain.

The quiet and tenuous hope expressed here is what we need—and nothing more would fit. I think of lines like Albany's, at the close of *King Lear:*

> The weight of this sad time we must obey;
> Speak what we feel, not what we ought to say.
> The oldest hath borne most; we that are young
> Shall never see so much nor live so long.

And that longevity of Lear's, of which Edgar speaks, is measured not just by his years, but by "the intensity of his existence."

The chorus's last lines in *Oedipus Rex* come to my mind also:

> Make way for Oedipus. All people said,
> "That is a fortunate man";
> And now what storms are beating on his head!
> Call no man fortunate that is not dead.
> The dead are free from pain.

A Man and His History

Ian Gregor

While his eyes were bent on the water beneath there slowly became visible a something floating in the circular pool formed by the wash of centuries; the pool he was intending to make his death-bed. At first it was indistinct by reason of the shadow from the bank; but it emerged thence and took shape, which was that of a human body, lying stiff and stark upon the surface of the stream.

In the circular current imparted by the central flow the form was brought forward, till it passed under his eyes; and then he perceived with a sense of horror that it was *himself.* Not a man somewhat resembling him, but one in all respects his counterpart, his actual double, was floating as if dead in Ten Hatches Hole.

In that memorable moment we find revealed an essential perspective for *The Mayor of Casterbridge.* No longer, as in *The Return of the Native,* is there "a dialogue of the mind with itself" expressed in diverse ways—the Heath, the acts of human desire, the self-conscious meditation on what the age demands—but rather a mute self-recognition, taking place within an individual consciousness fatally divided against itself. It was a shift which Hardy recognised in his preface to the novel: "The story," he writes, "is more particularly of one man's deeds and character than, perhaps, any other of those included in my Exhibition of Wessex life." "One man's deeds " is a phrase which describes the great

From *The Great Web: The Form of Hardy's Major Fiction.* © 1974 by Ian Gregor. Faber & Faber, 1974.

achievement—and the limitations—of the novel.

For Hardy, with *The Return of the Native* behind him, to be able to find in one man his governing interest suggests how richly he felt himself able to register a notion of "character," capable of containing within it all the essential interests so lavishly dispersed in the earlier novel. That is to say, we do not feel, as we move from one novel to the other, any narrowing of scope, any diminution in tragic scale. The title page defines the arena of dramatic interest—*The Life and Death of The Mayor of Casterbridge: A Story of a Man of Character.* In that tension between the public circumstances and the individual response, we have the dynamic of the novel. Continually, we are made aware of both elements operating throughout the novel, so that we cannot think of Henchard apart from his work, his work apart from the town, the town apart from the age, whether it is the age which "bespoke the art of Rome, concealed dead men of Rome," or the age which finds the town still just beyond the outstretched arm of the railway. But no more can we think of Henchard without hearing "a laugh not encouraging to strangers," without seeing a man "reckon his sacks by chalk strokes. . . measure his ricks by stretching with his arms," without feeling "the blazing regard" he gave to those who won his feelings. If we were to try to characterise the distinctiveness of this "one man" we might echo Kent's remark to Lear:

> "You have in your countenance that which I would fain
> cal master."
> "What's that?"
> "Authority."
>
> (act 1, scene 4)

In describing Henchard in these terms I am thinking more of the decisive imaginative impact he makes on the reader, than of the detail of his own personality. When we reflect on the latter, we are faced with sustained ambivalence. The adjectives crowd in to make their rival claims—egotistic, rash, jealous, generous, self-critical, honourable. And these claims are pressed home with force and precision—there are no half-measures, no truce between them.

If, however, we ponder the force that is "Henchard," we cannot really say that it arises from the interplay, however vigorous, of these various elements. We cannot, in other words, feel that he inhabits Hardy's imagination, and in turn ours, as a complex psychological figure. For Hardy, the imaginative pressure at work in the creation of Henchard is not expressed in individual analysis, but in terms of a series of actions whose effects can be neither determined nor confined. "One man's deeds" in this novel can contain the exploration of a community, not in the sense of its detail, but in the contrast between the solidity of its present and the haunting power of its past.

It is Hardy's ability to find within Henchard a multidimensional perspective which prompts the word "epic" as an appropriate descriptive term. The force that he exerts, the authority with which he speaks, these belong to someone who can be titled, with propriety, "The Mayor of Casterbridge," and in that role he can add a footnote to history, and play a part in a tragedy. But within the Mayor is the haytrusser, the man who sold his wife at a fair in a drunken stupor, who later deceived a father about the existence of his child so that "scarcely believing the evidence of his senses, (he) rose from his seat amazed at what he had done." For Hardy, then, to explore "the volcanic stuff beneath the rind" in Henchard, is to explore the whole area of conflict which so preoccupied him in *The Return of the Native:* the divisiveness of consciousness within man himself whereby his very energies become directed towards his self-destruction, and the relation of that consciousness to inevitable processes of change, whether these are seen in terms of society or in terms of nature. If we isolate any of these elements, so that we see Henchard as a psychological case study, or a tragic hero, or as the last representative in a changing agrarian order, we fail to do justice to Hardy's conception of character, to the fact that "one man's deeds" can serve as an "Exhibition of Wessex life." "Egdon," "Clym," "Eustacia"—all these elements are present in that confrontation Henchard has with "himself" in Ten Hatches Hole.

That Henchard should permit Hardy this inclusiveness of vision is certainly one of the triumphs of this novel; it is also its limitation. If we say that Henchard drains life out of the other characters, this is not to say that he is the only convincing character in the novel. Elizabeth-Jane, and certainly Farfrae, can be thought of as genuine presences. The way he affects the life of the other characters is in making us feel they are never allowed to live and breathe apart from him. At the level of plot, he systematically dismisses them from his life: Susan, Farfrae, Lucetta, Elizabeth—all are cut off from him as severely as he aims to cut himself off from the human community in the prescriptions of his Will.

In both Elizabeth and Farfrae we sense an intended elaboration of character which we can only observe through a glass darkly. Elizabeth's pursuit of learning is perfunctorily presented, her books become stage properties, her reunion with her father is hurriedly dismissed. Farfrae in his relationship with Henchard is skilfully presented; in his relationship with Lucetta and Elizabeth, he hardly exists. If it comes as a shock to read his reflection on Lucetta's death, "it was hard to believe that life with her would have been productive of further happiness," it is not so much because of its crude insensitivity, as because we realise that Farfrae's relationship with her has hardly been created for us at all. Newson only lives as a simple device of the plot, because for Henchard that is all he is. Susan's case is a particularly revealing one, as R. B. Heilman has pointed out in a shrewd essay on the novel. Heilman traces out her "career," that of one continuously presented as meek and barely competent; he concludes: "Hardy might well have told us about Susan's energy, spirit, inventiveness, native shrewdness amounting at times to foxiness, strategic sense and managerial skill little short of brilliant, and pointed out that she was one of the few women who get what they want." If Susan does not quite strike us in that way, Heilman's account makes us sharply aware how much we have become influenced by Henchard's reaction to her and how, indeed, he seems to have persuaded Hardy to connive in his account too. What all these incidents have in common is that all these characters draw their dramatic life directly from Henchard, and that once they become involved in scenes which do not concern him in any direct way, then they would seem to forfeit not only Henchard's interest but Hardy's also. It is wryly amusing to see that Henchard's power is such that it appears to cut the author off too, so that his occasional *obiter dicta* seem to italicise themselves awkwardly, and remain rather sour asides having little to do with the actual drama that is taking place.

It is, of course, the dominance of Henchard that causes Hardy to get into a great deal of trouble with his plotting in this novel; in order to keep it moving, he has to have recourse to letters which are not properly sealed, parcels which are badly packed, and conversations which are overheard. These always remain devices and have none of the resonance that so often accompanies Hardy's plotting. Hardy himself was very conscious of this defect in *The Mayor* and remarked that "it was a story which he had damaged more recklessly as an artistic whole . . . than perhaps any of his other novels." He attributes the damage to serial pressures, which had led him into over-plotting. This may have been the effect upon him, but the cause lay in the conception of a novel centred on "one man's deeds," which required leisurely development, careful distribution of interest, and a plot stripped of superfluous incident.

In beginning this chapter in this way I have tried to describe the dominant impression which I think *The Mayor of Casterbridge* could make on the reader, and I have set it out in this rather stark way at the outset because I think it can exert a misleading influence on our reading of the novel as a whole. The impression I have described centres on the force of Henchard's character and, as a corollary, the relative weakness of the other characters and the inadequacies of the plot. What makes that impression misleading is that it is too static; "character" for Hardy can never be seen in a tightly inclusive way, and plot is not to be identified with that sense of irresistible movement which is so powerful an element in this novel.

I shall try to illustrate this, first by examining the initial impression made by the novel in the opening two chapters, then by looking at a chapter where a significant development does take place, apart from Henchard, and finally, by looking at the closing two chapters where the novel finds its resolution.

II

The function of the opening two chapters is to initiate the action and to serve as an overture to the novel as a whole. Their subject matter is the arrival of Henchard with his wife at the Fair in Weydon-Priors; the selling of Susan to the sailor in a mood of drunken frustration; Henchard's recognition, the following day, of the terrible deed he has done; his solemn vow never to touch alcohol for twenty-one years, "being a year for every year I have lived"; and his setting off alone to Casterbridge to look for work and to begin a new life.

> One evening of late summer, before the nineteenth century had reached one-third of its span, a young man and woman, the latter carrying a child, were approaching the large village of Weydon-Priors, in Upper Wessex, on foot. They were plainly but not ill clad, though the thick hoar of dust which had accumulated on their shoes and garments from an obviously long journey lent a disadvantageous shabbiness to their appearance just now.

The novel opens in these classical cadences of "once upon a time." At the centre, taking the attention, is Henchard, at first sour and indifferent, then made quarrelsome and pugnacious by drink, then bewildered

but finally determined in his remorse. It is a kaleidoscope of moods all
being lived out at the nerve's end, and fuelling them all, there is a deep
and diffused sense of self-estrangement. Self-enclosed, his wife appears "to walk the highway alone, save for the child she bore." About
the family there is an "atmosphere of stale familiarity," and in Nature
too, life has faded, the leaves are "doomed" and "blackened green,"
the "grassy margins of the bank" are "powdered by dust." The mood
is suggestive of that described by Donne in "The Nocturnall upon St.
Lucie's Day" :

> The world's whole sap is sunke:
> The generall balm the hydroptique earth hath drunk,
> Whither, as to the bed's-feet, life is shrunke.

That is the general mood of these opening pages; Henchard's particular
mood is more difficult to define. We feel in it bafflement, frustration, a
sense that life has possibilities which have been denied him. It is interesting that the very first words which are spoken in the novel, the first
gesture towards self-fulfilment, takes the form of the question "Any
trade doing here?" It is the sense of the centrality of work in finding
fulfilment that is such a major preoccupation of this novel.

As soon as we put it that way we can see what a rare novel *The
Mayor of Casterbridge* is in the history of English fiction, where the
model of self-fulfilment is found, invariably, in personal relationships.
If we think of Lawrence, a novelist who comes very close to Hardy in
many ways, and think of the self-estrangement of Tom Brangwen and
the self-estrangement of Henchard, the rarity of Hardy's position becomes plain. *The Mayor* is an intensely public novel in its drive; how
public can be gauged from the fact that it must be one of the very few
major novels—or for that matter, very few novels—where sexual relationships are not, in one way or another, the dominant element. That
Hardy can write a novel which engages his full imaginative range
without making us feel the relative absence of such relationships, suggests that it is not the individual human heart which beats at the centre of
his fictional world.

The marriage that is broken at Weydon-Priors is not, so far as
Hardy is concerned, an individual affair. In these opening chapters we
move steadily away from the individual—we are never, at any point,
taken "inside" Henchard—to the world in which he is finding it difficult to make a living, the world of houses being pulled down and
people having nowhere to go. There is the voice of the auctioneer sell-

ing off the last of the horses and gradually insinuating into Henchard's mind a wish to start again, to shake himself free from all encumbrance, to sell his wife. Susan is sold at a strange dreamlike auction in which there are no bidders, but the price goes up and up. I think it is possible to make too much of the particulars of this vivid and bizarre scene, so that the whole emphasis falls on the act of selling itself, the reduction of a person to a commodity. But Hardy's interests are not those, say, of James in *The Spoils of Poynton*. His eye is not so much on money, as on the notion of "freedom" it appears to offer, and which Henchard is so intent on grasping, "if I were a free man again I'd be worth a thousand pound before I'd done o't." That is the sentence which catches the undercurrent of meditation that runs persistently through the chapter, the keenly felt "if I were." It is that sentiment which is present in the visitation of the late swallow finding its way into the tent, like the men who watch it, "absently," a migrant, but unlike them free in a way they can never be. This meditative note is struck most firmly at the end of the chapter when we are taken outside the tent, and the sight of the horses "crossing their necks and rubbing each other lovingly" is set in contrast to the harsh act of humanity we have just witnessed. But, immediately, that note is played in a different key: we are asked to reflect on the occasions when humanity sleeps innocently while inanimate nature rages round him. And there at the end of the paragraph we find an unobtrusive phrase which gives us bearings on the whole scene— "all terrestrial conditions were intermittent." In other words those who seek to impress themselves on the universe, to lay violent hands on time, to forget that man is the slave of limit—such men can only succeed in destroying themselves. They will be extinguished as surely as the last candle is, when the furmity seller goes out to leave Henchard alone in the tent sunk in a drunken sleep.

But for Hardy flux is always followed by reflux, an essential element in his narrative compulsion, no less than in his metaphysical outlook. Chapter 1 then tells for Hardy precisely half of the human story; chapter 2 reverses the emphasis and, in so doing, tells the other half.

Henchard is again at the centre, Henchard now waking to find "the morning sun" streaming through the crevices. Outside, "the freshness of the September morning inspired and braced him as he stood." He can see far across the valleys "dotted with barrows, and trenched with . . . prehistoric forts." *This* is a world upon which man has impressed himself, so that "the whole scene lay under the rays of a newly risen sun, which had not as yet dried a single blade of the heavily

dewed grass." The voice of the weak bird of the previous night singing "a trite old evening song" gives way to "the yellow-hammers
which flitted about the hedges with straws in their bills." This vitality
and purposiveness encompasses Henchard too.

The previous night he sought to set aside time, to disown his past;
now he will bind himself to time, more, he will mortgage his future.
He gave himself away in a drunken stupor in a furmity tent, now in
recollecting himself he swears his great vow on the clamped book
which lies on the communion table in a nearby village church. Instinctively, he seeks a ritual gesture, "a fit place and imagery," which will
release him from the thraldom of the moment. "He shouldered his basket
and moved on"—that is the driving sentiment of this second chapter.
Purposeful and resilient, Henchard has now a full consciousness of his
position. He tries, without success, to find his wife and family and then,
learning of their emigration, "he said he would search no longer . . . .
Next day he started, journeying southwestward, and did not pause,
except for nights' lodgings, till he reached the town of Casterbridge,
in a far distant part of Wessex." In that closing sentence of the chapter
we hear the classical cadences of the archetypal story, present in the
opening paragraph, announce themselves again. And it is to be there,
in Casterbridge, that the complementary tensions so explicitly set up
in these two opening chapters will be developed and pursued.

"A series of seemings"—the opening of *The Mayor of Casterbridge*
reveals, in a remarkably pure way, the characteristic Hardy stance
towards experience. Within each chapter a set of reverberations is released from a single violent act—the sale of the wife, Henchard's vow.
A perspective on the human deed is established. The act of an individual
person cannot be contained by that individual life; it leads persistently
outwards to the whole social context, a context both personal and social,
as the full title of the novel we are considering makes plain: *The Life and
Death of the Mayor of Casterbridge*. The "seemings" are here, but in
themselves they don't constitute the shape of a life. They are true to
consciousness heightened in moments of vision; they fail to do justice to
consciousness as continually present, continually altering. It is here that
"series" has its part to play, with its emphasis on process and continuity.

In the aesthetic structure of a Hardy novel the tension between the
terms is expressed in the dynamic interplay between plot and image,
and encompassing both is the compassionate presence of the narrator,
whose mediating consciousness is an integral part of the drama he is
concerned to reveal. In the very elements which go to make up his

fiction—the narrative trajectory, the sudden moment of symbolic concentration, the oscillations between story and commentary—in all of these elements, Hardy is acting out his own impression of life as a series of seemings, and the novelist's art is here not simply to reveal but to enact it. In particular terms, this is communicated most frequently in that air of ambivalence which hangs over so many incidents in the novel, an ambivalence which creates in the reader not so much an awareness of complexity as a desire to suspend judgement and to sense a more inclusive view.

It is an air which is strongly present in the presentation of Casterbridge itself. Our first glimpse of the town is in lamplight "through the engirdling trees, conveying a sense of great snugness and comfort inside." But to the eyes of the travelled, if inexperienced, Elizabeth-Jane it already seems "an old-fashioned place." Hardy holds a delicate balance in his initial presentation of Casterbridge between the warm nostalgia prompted by his boyhood memories of Dorchester in the 1840s and the reflections of an adult already aware of its remoteness, its inability to adapt itself to a changing world. "Country and town met at a mathematical line"—it is like a child's drawing, and like such a drawing exhibits its own charm, its own falsity. The town's band may be shaking the windows with "The Roast Beef of Old England," Henchard may be reintroduced to us through his laughter, but outside in the streets, the newly arrived wayfarers hear that he has overreached himself: he has sold "blown wheat," and there has never been such "unprincipled bread in Casterbridge before." The adjective does more than catch the vivacity of dialect, it casts a sardonic eye on one aspect at least of the Mayor's rise to prosperity. To the wayfarers, Casterbridge offers "a sense of great snugness and comfort," but to Buzzford, the local dealer, it is "a old hoary place o'wickedness."

From the outset of the novel the reader is made quietly aware of ambivalence, and aware of it as arising from "the way things are" rather than through the artifice of the novelist. Consider the relatively unobtrusive, but significant, play which is made of Farfrae's songs of home. The tone is lightly ironical at the expense of a man who looks back fondly on a country he has certainly no wish to return to; but at the same time, his sentiments are expressed in song, indicative of his resilience, his desire to travel, the ease he feels in company, and the unfeigned pleasure he gives to others. As the rivalry between Farfrae and Henchard builds up, we feel the same duality of feeling present, so that when Abel Whittle is reprimanded for his lateness at work, we feel

Henchard's treatment is concerned, but humiliating, Farfrae's impersonal but just. In the rival entertainments they set up for the town, Henchard is bountiful but patronising, Farfrae cannily prudent, but infectiously ingenious.

The oscillation of sympathy is not confined to the main action. It is present in that fine town-pump chat which followed the death of Susan Henchard. "She was as white as marble-stone," says Mrs. Cuxom with evident relish, as she proceeds to relay the details of Susan's preparations for her burial. "Ah, poor heart!"—and a general sigh goes up. Then suddenly the tone changes from elegy to indignation. Christopher Coney has removed the pennies from the dead woman's eyes and spent them at The Three Mariners. " 'Faith,' he said, 'why should death rob life o' fourpence. . . money is scarce and throats get dry.' " Beneath the humour a genuine point is being made. Just as suddenly the tone shifts back again, not to the gossipy note of concern with which the conversation began, but to an impersonal note of elegy, which both pays tribute to Susan and also recognises the substance in Coney's remark, though without approving his action:

> "Well, poor soul; she's helpless to hinder that or anything now," answered Mother Cuxom. "And all her shining keys will be took from her, and her cupboards opened; and little things a' didn't wish seen, anybody will see; and her wishes and ways will all be as nothing."

It is a small incident, existing in the margin of the main action, but like Abel Whittle's speech about the death of Henchard in the last chapter, making the grain of the novel suddenly glow—the cadence may point to the inevitable obliterations of time, but there, in the centre, taking the eye, hard and personal, are Susan's "shining keys."

All this indicates something of the distinctive rhythm of the novel; but before looking at the resolutions towards which it moves, I would like to examine a chapter which exists almost at the very centre of the novel. I emphasise the word "chapter" here because it is the rhythm established by the aesthetic unit that I wish to draw attention to. It is chapter 24 and the subject matter is simply told.

Lucetta, now a lady of means, and Elizabeth-Jane are regarding the affairs of the Casterbridge marketplace. From Lucetta's window they can observe the varied activity, and one day they see the arrival of a new seed-drill. Going out into the marketplace to satisfy their curiosity, they find its arrival due to Farfrae, who is busy examining and displaying it. Hesitantly, the two women meet Henchard, who is also looking at the machine, and there is a sardonic exchange about the latest innovation. Both women are made increasingly conscious of their emotional involvements. Elizabeth, isolated from her father, has a growing sense of Lucetta's fascination with Farfrae. Lucetta admits as much, and the episode closes with an oblique attempt on her part to seek Elizabeth's advice.

Even from such a summary as this it is clear that Hardy, in a sure and economical way, is securing the interpenetration of the public and private themes of the novel and bringing them into sharp focus, almost wittily, in Farfrae's singing his romantic song of exile from inside the new agricultural machine. As he sings about Kitty "wi' a braw new gown," we remember that Lucetta is also wearing a new gown which alone rivalled the machine in colour. New machines, new London fashions: the complementary development is made. Lucetta looking at her gown spread out on the bed chooses "to be the cherry-coloured person at all hazards" as surely as Mixen Lane will choose that particular gown to identify her in the skimmity-ride. These are ironies of a now familiar kind, but what ought to take our attention in this chapter is not the oscillation of feeling, but a point of growth, a decisive move forward in the articulation of the novel.

The chapter opens with the phrase "Poor Elizabeth-Jane," and it closes with the sentence "For by the 'she' of Lucetta's story Elizabeth had not been beguiled." The decisive move in this chapter lies not in the scene contemplated from the window or in the marketplace, sharp and vivacious as it is, but in Hardy's creation of "a contemplative eye" for Elizabeth. He is in the delicate process in this chapter of merging the authorial consciousness of the veiled narrator with that of Elizabeth. Hinted parallels between the artist's eye and Elizabeth's begin to be made. We are told that the marketplace offers itself to the House like a stage for a drama, and when Elizabeth reacts to the new seed-drill it is in a very literary manner. Responding to Farfrae's enthusiasm about its efficiency she says, "Then the romance of the sower is gone . . ." and then, more characteristically, "How things change!" It is worth observing the reactions of Farfrae and Lucetta to this. Farfrae says, "But the machines are already very common in the East and North of England." And Lucetta, whose acquaintance with Scripture is, as Hardy says, "somewhat limited," remarks admiringly and practically, "Is the machine yours?" It is a small exchange, but it neatly conveys a new authorial relationship to "poor Elizabeth-Jane." This, of course, is given a decisive orientation at the end of the chapter when Elizabeth is asked to respond to Lucetta's carefully contrived story of her past. She has no difficulty in interpreting its true meaning. Interpreting, but not condemning, this provides her initiation into sympathetic detachment, beginning paradoxically with her own increasing emotional involvement with Lucetta and with Farfrae. And in that paradox Elizabeth is revealing herself not simply as a companion for Lucetta, but as a companion for Hardy too. In chapter 24 we have a decisive step in her education: she is to learn the distinction between the fictive world and the real one, Newson's daughter, not Henchard's.

The full importance of Elizabeth's role, which begins to appear in this chapter, becomes quite clear in the final chapters of the novel. Hardy is going to need her "quiet eye" less in the dramatic unfolding of the tale—though she has her small part to play here too—than as a way of enabling us to understand its resolution. It is a resolution which will involve the most dramatic nuancing of "the series of seemings," and which will incorporate the developed consciousness of Elizabeth-Jane as part of its meaning.

The last two chapters stand in the same dramatic relationship to the novel as the first two. The main action is completed and the centre of our attention is Henchard—once more a wayfarer and a haytrusser. "He could not help thinking of Elizabeth"—that is the dominant mood of the penultimate chapter, everything else takes its bearings from that. But first Henchard must encounter his past again. He returns to the hill at Weydon-Priors where the furmity tent had stood twenty-five years previously, "Here we went in, and here we sat down." With absorbed intentness he recreates the scene of his crime and the authorial voice lends him support: "And thus Henchard found himself again on the precise standing which he had occupied a quarter of a century earlier. Externally there was nothing to hinder his making another start on the upward slope." But it is too late in the day for that. Haunted by thoughts of Elizabeth in Casterbridge, he hears that arrangements have been made for her wedding to Farfrae, and he resolves to return for the occasion. Delaying his arrival until the festivities are well under way, he makes himself known at the house, after unobtrusively leaving his gift in the garden—a caged goldfinch. It is the first time he has met Elizabeth since she discovered that Henchard had delayed Newson's return to her. Face to face now, he seeks forgiveness, but she rejects him, and without any further defence of his conduct he bids her a final farewell and goes out into the night.

It is interesting to recall that it was this chapter which Hardy decided to omit from the first edition of the novel, fearing that Henchard's return to Elizabeth would weaken the final effect of the tragedy. Hardy was prevailed upon to restore the chapter, and this was done for the 1895 edition. And rightly, because its inclusion gives the emphasis to two essential elements in the conclusion of the novel. The first is the force given to Henchard's isolation from the community, not simply by a kind of muted withdrawal, but by rejection. The second is the creation of a reverse effect. Elizabeth's life with Farfrae is, we must feel assured, to be one of happiness. Whatever happens to Henchard that relationship will prosper in its own quiet way. And so we find the chapter reaching out towards that balance of contraries so characteristic of the novel as a whole. And reaching out in a way that quite naturally will employ the rhetoric which conveys a classical ending to an archetypal story—the marriage and wedding feast on the one hand, the exclusion of the disruptive force on the other.

But Hardy distrusts this kind of finality, this confident distribution of sympathy. And so in his final chapter Hardy is concerned to deindividualise his novel, to distance its themes. There is a moment in the penultimate chapter where we can see the kind of temptation which hovered over the ending, a temptation to go for emotional "bravura." Henchard's wedding gift to Elizabeth, the caged goldfinch, remains an unfocused poignancy—the size of the gesture concealing its imprecision, so that if it is meant as some kind of symbolic expression about Henchard's fate, we remain uneasy as to whether the expression is Henchard's or Hardy's. I draw attention to the goldfinch only to show how sure Hardy's touch is in the remainder of the last chapter, where there is no forced symbolism of any kind, nothing mawkish in a situation where that tone is difficult to resist. And, when we consider that the chapter is written from the vantage point of a worried and remorseful daughter, the achievement becomes all the more remarkable.

It is the discovery of the bird-cage which sets Elizabeth and Farfrae off to look for Henchard. If it is Casterbridge and the wedding feast which set the mood for the preceding chapter, so now, in the last chapter, it is the heath and an isolated hut which "of humble dwellings was surely the humblest." Henchard has returned to a tract of land "whose surface never had been stirred to a finger's depth, save by the scratching of rabbits, since brushed by the feet of the earliest tribes." In this sense everything is to be stripped to essentials, the world which is to be seen by the travellers is a moral landscape as well as a natural one, and we are moved to see, in Wordsworth's phrase, into "the life of things." Characteristically, on this bedrock of human experience, Hardy continues his contraries.

The perspective the Heath offers is one of timeless change, the endless ebb and flow of human existence, stretching back to a limitless past, forward to a limitless future. At the centre, two wayfarers pursue a difficult search. The scene offers itself irresistibly as an image of our terrestrial condition. Then, suddenly, casually, a figure appears, Abel Whittle, whose only role in the novel so far has been to provide the first occasion when Henchard and Farfrae clashed. And now—like Mother Cuxom on the death of Susan—it is this marginal figure who is chosen to express, in one of the most moving passages of the novel, the contrary perspective to that proffered by the Heath. Comparison has sometimes been made between Whittle's role here and that of the Fool in *King Lear.* Like the larger comparison, the smaller is wide of the mark. The Fool proffers "wisdom," a self-conscious commentary on Lear's plight. Whittle offers the purest form of human gesture, the instinctual made sublime by its disinterestedness, "ye wer kind-like to mother if ye were rough to me, and I would fain be kind-like to you." It is "love thy neighbour as thyself," presented with total dramatic simplicity and conviction. It is the felicity of "kind-like" with all its overtures of kinship and kindred, that demands, in Hardy's eyes, no less recognition as part of our terrestrial condition than the humbling perspectives suggested by the Heath. In Henchard's Will we find the confluence of these views. There is the wish for annihilation in death, "that no man remember me"; there is also the unshakable belief in the personal rightness of the testimony, "To this I put my name—Michael Henchard," just as twenty-five years before, "Dropping his head upon the clamped book which lay on the Communion-table, he said aloud —'I, Michael Henchard.' " It is a perspective which resists challenge and remains untouched by irony, Hardy's sense of "a man of character."

For Henchard life has been tragic, but never at any time has it lost dignity and it is this which Elizabeth responds to when she comes finally to mediate this experience for us. The Heath, Able Whittle—the contraries caught here are too intense for the ebb and flow of ordinary lives. It is "the ordinary" Elizabeth offers. When she responds to Henchard's Will it is not to the prescriptions, but to the knowledge that "the man who wrote them meant what he said . . . (they) were not to be tampered with to give herself a mournful pleasure, or her husband credit for large-heartedness." She disclaims "mournful pleasures," and with Henchard's life now behind her she is given full liberty to reflect. It is a reflection which attempts to render continual justice to the contraries of existence, to the series of seemings, as these make themselves felt in the last, and much misunderstood, sentence of the novel:

> And in being forced to class herself among the fortunate she did not cease to wonder at the persistence of the unforeseen, when the one to whom such unbroken tranquillity had been accorded in the adult stage was she whose youth had seemed to teach that happiness was but the occasional episode in a general drama of pain.

How often the final phrase has been wrenched from its context and made to do duty for a view not only of this novel, but of the general tenor of Hardy's fiction. "The persistence of the unforeseen," it is this phrase which mobilises the paragraph, keeps the contraries open, and is as resistant to a view of life as "a general drama of pain" as it is to one of "unbroken tranquillity." Elizabeth's eye—and Hardy's too—is on the wonder of change here, on flux and reflux, putting her youth beside her "adult stage," not intent on finding in those phases prescriptions for life in general. It is not simply the unseen that keeps us alert to such change, but its *persistence:* it is this which becomes part of the fabric of everyday living. At times, Henchard had tried to separate out the unseen from that fabric and to live by it, and the past and the future devoured his present; at times, Farfrae was so totally absorbed by the fabric that being out on the heath was being "reduced," and staying overnight there a matter of making "a hole in a sovereign." Elizabeth, like Thomas in *The Return of the Native,* accepts the Heath, and the drama it has witnessed, calmly, and for what it is, neither an implacable force nor a backdrop to man's desires.

III

If at the end of *The Mayor of Casterbridge* Elizabeth leaves us thinking about the relation of past to present, we are taken back to consider an issue which I considered at the beginning of this chapter, Hardy's sense of man-in-history, and the way in which this is present in *The Mayor of Casterbridge.*

The preface which Hardy wrote for the 1895 edition reminds us directly of this:

> The incidents narrated arise mainly out of three events, which chanced to range themselves in the order and at or about the intervals of time here given, in the real history of the town called Casterbridge.... They were the sale of a wife by her husband, the uncertain harvests which immediately preceded the repeal of the Corn Laws, and the visit of a Royal Personage to the aforesaid part of England.

Of these, the first and third have little literary-critical interest, though as always it is interesting to watch Hardy, particularly in the case of the wife-sale, feel the necessity of validating its inclusion by reference to factual circumstances. He would appear to have come across several instances in the pages of the *Dorset County Chronicle,* which he began to read in 1884 in preparation for his novel. Beginning with the issues of January 1826, he read through the files in a systematic way as far as late 1829 or early 1830. In the course of this reading he discovered no less than three instances of wife-selling, one of the most relevant of which reads:

> *Selling Wife:* At Buckland, nr. Frome, a labring (sic) man named Charles Pearce sold wife to shoemaker named Elton for £5 and delivered her in a halter in the public street. She seemed very willing. Bells rang.

It is an incident which Hardy's love of the factually bizarre would find highly congenial, but it was a remarkable sense of confidence that allowed him to open the novel with this incident, and give it the tragic, as distinct from the merely bizarre, resonance which he needed.

The appearance of the Royal Personage sits very lightly to Hardy's main interests in the novel. It would seem almost certain that the reference was to Prince Albert who passed through Dorchester in July 1849 on his way to Weymouth to lay the foundation stone of Portland Breakwater. The incident obviously provided Hardy with an opportunity for parodying pomp and circumstance, and, more to his interest, for showing the blight that ran throughout Casterbridge, so that the preparations being made in the Council Chamber for the Royal visit occur simultaneously with the preparations being made in Mixen Lane for the skimmity-ride. But this kind of social satire engages Hardy's attention only lightly, and it is difficult not to regard the whole episode as one of those which he felt had been forced upon him by the constant demand made by the serial form for continuous plotting.

The third factor which Hardy draws attention to in his preface, the repeal of the Corn Laws, is very different in importance. Indeed, it has an importance which has influenced the way the novel, as a whole, has been read. It shapes, for instance, the kind of reading which Douglas Brown offers in his perceptive study of Hardy:

> *The Mayor of Casterbridge,* then, is the tale of the struggle between the native countryman and the alien invader; of the defeat of dull courage and traditional attitudes by insight, craft and the vicissitudes of nature; and of the persistence through that defeat of some deep layer of vitality in the country protagonist. . . . *The Mayor of Casterbridge* turns on the situation that led to the repeal of the Corn Laws. The consequences of that repeal to Victorian agricultural life are the centre of this book, provide the impulse that makes it what it is.

"The native countryman," "the alien invader"—this is the kind of polarity that a concentration on the phrase "the repeal of the Corn Laws" can lead to, so that Brown can go on to say that the consequences of the repeal are "the centre of the book." But, as Hardy's preface makes clear, he is not talking about the repeal of the Corn Laws as such; his emphasis is on "the uncertain harvests which immediately preceded their repeal," and his emphasis will not really encourage a reading of the novel which sees it in terms of a polarising conflict between "the native countryman" and "the alien invader."

If we look at "the native countryman" we find a good deal that is less flattering than "dull courage"; he is tetchy, grasping, superstitious, and indifferent to any consequences beyond the immediate present. If we look at "the alien invader" we find that, so far from invading the community, he actually joins it (a point which Brown concedes in a later account of the novel without, however, feeling that this calls for an overall revision of his general reading), and indeed Farfrae goes on to give it whatever prosperity it can obtain. If we are concerned with the Corn Laws at all directly in this novel then, as J. C. Maxwell has pointed out, Hardy is going out of his way, in his remark about "the uncertain harvests," to indicate that he is choosing "the *latest* period at which the uncushioned dominance of price fluctuations depending on the home harvest . . . still persisted." In other words, far from presenting an innocent agrarian economy undermined by new grasping business methods, Hardy shows in Henchard (if we really want to talk in these terms) the last of the old profiteers, existing by courtesy of a closed system of economic protection. With the repeal of the Corn Laws, the local weather ceased to exert its tyranny on the market, and Farfrae certainly began to prosper by "canny moderation"; but as Maxwell remarks, it is really Henchard's colleagues who are "the lineal descendents of Shakespeare's farmer who hanged himself on the expectation of plenty."

Clearly, it would be absurd to read the novel in such a way as to make it an indictment of Henchard and a vindication of Farfrae. I have put the counter-case simply to show that when concentration is made too directly on the historical implications of the novel, so that we see a precise agricultural crisis constituting its "centre," then the move takes us further and further away from its imaginative life.

The sense in which history is deeply meaningful in *the Mayor of Casterbridge* can be suggested, I think, by looking at a passage which captures with some of the intensity of his lyric poetry a basic apprehension about the passage of time. Elizabeth has been sitting up through the night looking after her mother who is dying:

> the silence in Casterbridge—barring the rare sound of the watchman—was broken in Elizabeth's ear only by the time-piece in the bedroom ticking frantically against the clock on the stairs; ticking harder and harder till it seemed to clang like a gong; and all this while the subtle-souled girl asking herself why she was born, why sitting in a room, and blinking at the candle; why things around her had taken the shape they wore in preference to every other possible shape. Why they stared at her so helplessly, as if waiting for the touch of some wand that should release them from terrestrial constraint; what that chaos called consciousness, which spun in her at this moment like a top, tended to, and began in. Her eyes fell together; she was awake, yet she was asleep.

That is a moment of imaginative distillation in the novel. "The subtle-souled girl" has little reality for us; it is rather the author caught reflecting on the nature of the imagination itself. Elizabeth is caught suspended between two levels of reality, so that she becomes the subject and object of her own perceptions. Withdrawing from the particularities of the scene about her, the girl knows a moment of heightened consciousness, but the intensity brings with it its own chaos, and then it subsides into the forgetfulness of sleep. The paragraph links time with consciousness, and that link is built into the very shape the novel takes.

"What is your history?" the question Lucetta puts to Elizabeth, is a question which Hardy puts to the reader, puts to himself, and puts to his characters. The way in which it is put to the reader is to be found in the opening paragraph of the preface:

> Readers of the following story who have not yet arrived at middle age are asked to bear in mind that, in the days recalled by the tale, the home Corn Trade, on which so much of the action turns, had an importance that can hardly be realized by those accustomed to the sixpenny loaf of the present date, and to the present indifference of the public to harvest weather.

"The days recalled . . . the present date," the whole novel was coloured by that interplay for Hardy's readers and it gave depth to its meaning. With time's lengthening perspective *The Mayor of Casterbridge* takes its place as a Hardy novel of the mid-1880s, but we should remember that for Hardy and his readers this was "a historical novel" about the 1840s, and more briefly, about the 1820s. We get something of the effect if we imagine ourselves reading in the 1970s a story set in the 1930s, whose opening lies in the years immediately preceding the First World War. It is the layering of time, the years between, that help to create the perspective within which we read, and extend the novelist's meaning. By the 1880s readers really *are* aware of the consequences of the repeal of the Corn Laws, the agricultural depression created by the importation of wheat from across the Atlantic really has affected the domestic market, and Farfrae's career for good or for ill can already be thought of as completed. But this is not a perspective which is sardonic. Hardy's eye, like Elizabeth's at the end of the novel, is on change, on flux and reflux; it is that idea that the dates are there to suggest, rather than any particular events with which they might be associated. Thus, the question "What is your history?" has a personal significance, as well as a public one. The author, in recalling the Dorchester of the 1840s, is recalling the period of his own boyhood, and the novel is as much concerned with recapturing the feeling of that period, as it is with charting social and economic change. Hence—we might go on to say—the deliberate blur that Hardy creates over a precise chronological scheme.

Implicit in memory for Hardy is tension, the inevitable tension between past and present; and this applies not only to the reader's experience of the novel and to the author's experience of writing it but also to the characters within it—most noticeably of course, to Henchard. Here again we have a history which is both public and private. It is public in the clash of interests between Henchard and Farfrae, a clash suitably described by the townspeople when they say of Henchard that "His accounts were like a bramblewood when Mr. Farfrae came. He used to reckon his sacks by chalk strokes all in a row like garden-palings, measure his ricks by stretching with his arms, weigh his trusses by a lift, judge his hay by a chaw, and settle the price with a curse. But now this accomplished young man does it all by ciphering and mensuration." That is the notion of change which belongs to the public history of the nineteenth century.

But the notion of history has for Henchard another, more urgent aspect. Henchard is looking at his daughter asleep: "He steadfastly regarded her features. . . . In sleep there come to the surface buried genealogical facts, ancestral curves, dead men's traits, which the mobility of daytime animation screens and overwhelms. . . . He could not endure the sight of her and hastened away." It is the hunger of a father for a child which he wants to claim as his own. Henchard's feeling for Elizabeth moves from that moment of anger when Susan takes her away, "She'd no business to take the maid—'tis my maid," to that moment of renunciation when he leaves her to Farfrae and goes to make his Will. That is a moment which could find suitable expression in lines from Eliot's "Marina," even though the mood which prompts them is very different:

> This form, this face, this life
> Living to live in a world of time beyond me; let me
> Resign my life for this life.

This is a longing inseparable from the needs of the human heart and such a coming to terms with change constitutes, for Hardy, a profound wisdom.

As we ponder this sense of a public and a private history we become aware that the particular tension which this novel describes works to keep them distinct from one another. On the one side, there is the element of "work," on the other, the element of "love." What is absent is that sense of interrelatedness presented most clearly in sexual relationships. There is passion in *The Mayor of Casterbridge,* but it is the passion of individual assertion, a passion which finds an appropriate epigraph in the phrase "A Man and His History." It is precisely this element of human relatedness which is to preoccupy Hardy in the remainder of the Wessex novels, and from *The Woodlanders* onwards sexual and economic possession will be seen as different aspects of a common process, so that in *Tess of the D'Urbervilles,* Hardy will find a history which is neither public nor private, but both, in the human body itself.

The Unmanning of the Mayor of Casterbridge

Elaine Showalter

To the feminist critic, Hardy presents an irresistible paradox. He is one of the few Victorian male novelists who wrote in what may be called a female tradition; at the beginning of his career, Hardy was greeted with the same uncertainty that had been engendered by the pseudonymous publication of *Jane Eyre* and *Adam Bede:* was the author man or woman? *Far from the Madding Crowd,* serialised in the *Cornhill* in 1874, was widely attributed to George Eliot, and Leslie Stephen wrote reassuringly to Hardy about the comparisons: "As for the supposed affinity to George Eliot, it consists, I think, simply in this that you have both treated rustics of the farming class in a humorous manner—Mrs. Poyser would be home I think, in Weatherbury—but you need not be afraid of such criticisms. You are original and can stand on your own legs."

It hardly needs to be said that Stephen's assessment of Hardy's originality was correct; but on the other hand, the relationship to Eliot went beyond similarities in content to similarities in psychological portraits, especially of women. Hardy's remarkable heroines, even in the earlier novels, evoked comparisons with Charlotte Brontë, Jane Austen, and George Eliot, indicating a recognition (as Havelock Ellis pointed out in his 1883 review-essay) that "the most serious work in modern English fiction. . .has been done by women." Later, Hardy's heroines spoke even more directly to women readers; after the publication of *Tess of the D'Urbervilles,* for example, Hardy received letters from wives who had not dared to tell their husbands about their premarital experience; sometimes these women requested meetings which he turned down on his barrister's advice. Twentieth-century criticism has often focused on the heroines of the novels; judging from the annual *Dissertation Abstracts* (Ann Arbor, Michigan) this perennial favourite of dissertation topics has received new incentive from the women's movement. Recent feminist criticism, most notably the distinguished essays of Mary Jacobus on Tess and Sue, has done much to unfold the complexities of Hardy's imaginative response to the "woman question" of the 1890s. Hardy knew and respected many of the minor women novelists of his day: Katherine Macquoid, Rhoda Broughton, Mary Braddon, Sarah Grand, Mona Caird, Evelyn Sharp, Charlotte Mew. He actually collaborated on a short story with the novelist Florence Henniker, and possibly revised the work of other female protegées; his knowledge of the themes of feminist writing in the 1880s and 1890s was extensive.

Yet other aspects of Hardy's work reveal a much more distanced and divided attitude towards women, a sense of an irreconcilable split between male and female values and possibilities. If some Victorian women recognised themselves in his heroines, others were shocked and indignant. In 1890, Hardy's friend Edmund Gosse wrote: "The unpopularity of Mr. Hardy's novels among women is a curious phenomenon. If he had no male admirers, he could almost cease to exist. . . . Even educated women approach him with hesitation and prejudice." Hardy hoped that *Tess of the D'Urbervilles* would redeem him; he wrote to Edmund Yates in 1891 that "many of my novels have suffered so much from misrepresentation as being attacks on womankind." He took heart from letters from mothers who were "putting 'Tess' into their daughters' hands to safeguard their future," and from "women of society" who said his courage had " done the whole sex a service." Gosse, however, read the hostile and uncomprehending reviews of such women as Margaret Oliphant as evidence of a continuing division between feminist critics, who were "shrivelled spinsters," and the "serious male public." There were indeed real and important ideological differences between Hardy and even advanced women of the 1890s, differences which Gosse wished to reduce to questions of sexual prudery. Hardy's emphasis on the biological determinism of childbearing, rather than on the economic determinants of female dependency, put him more in the camp of Grant Allen than in the women's party. In 1892 he declined membership in the Women's Progressive Society because he had not "as yet been converted to a belief in the desirability of the Society's first object"—women's suffrage. By 1906 his conversion had taken place; but his support of the suffrage campaign was based on his hope (as he wrote to Millicent Garrett Fawcett) that "the tendency of the women's vote will be to break up the present pernicious conventions in respect of manners, customs, religion, illegitimacy, the stereotyped household (that it must be the unit of society), the father of a woman's child (that it is anybody's business but the woman's own except in cases of disease or insanity)."

Looking at the novels of the 1890s, and at Hardy's treatment of his heroines as they encounter pernicious conventions, A. O. J. Cockshut has concluded that there were unbridgeable gaps between Hardy's position and that of fin-de-siècle feminism:

> Hardy decisively rejects the whole feminist argument of the preceding generation, which was the soil for the growth of the idea of the "New Woman" à la Havelock Ellis and Grant Allen; and this is his final word on the matter. The feminists saw the natural disabilities as trivial compared with those caused by bad traditions and false theories. Hardy reversed this, and he did so feelingly. The phrase "inexorable laws of nature" was no cliché for him. It represented the slowly-garnered fruits of his deepest meditations on life. It was an epitome of what found full imaginative expression in memorable descriptions, like that of Egdon Heath. The attempt to turn Hardy into a feminist is altogether vain.
>
> (*Man and Woman: A Study of Love and the Novel 1740–1940*)

But the traditional attention to Hardy's heroines has obscured other themes of equal significance to a feminist critique. Through the heroes of his novels and short stories, Hardy also investigated the Victorian codes of manliness, the man's experience of marriage, the problem of paternity. For the heroes of the tragic novels—Michael Henchard, Jude Fawley, Angel Clare—maturity involves a kind of assimilation of female suffering, an identification with a woman which is also an effort to come to terms with their own deepest selves. In Hardy's career too there is a consistent element of self-expression through women; he uses them as narrators, as secretaries, as collaborators, and finally, in the (auto) biography he wrote in the persona of his second wife, as screens or ghosts of himself. Hardy not only commented upon, and in a sense, infiltrated, feminine fictions; he also understood the feminine self as the estranged and essential complement of the male self. In *The Mayor of Casterbridge* (1886), Hardy gives the fullest nineteenth-century portrait of a man's inner life—his rebellion and his suffering, his loneliness and jealousy, his paranoia and despair, his uncontrollable unconscious. Henchard's efforts, first to deny and divorce his passional self, and ultimately to accept and educate it, involve him in a pilgrimage of "unmanning" which is a movement towards both self-discovery and tragic vulnerability. It is in the analysis of this New Man, rather than in the evaluation of Hardy's New Women, that the case for Hardy's feminist sympathies may be argued.

The Mayor of Casterbridge begins with a scene that dramatises the analysis of female subjugation as a function of capitalism which Engels had recently set out in *The Origins of the Family, Private Property and the State* (1884): the auction of Michael Henchard's wife Susan at the fair at Weydon-Priors. Henchard's drunken declaration that Susan is his "goods" is matched by her simple acceptance of a new "owner," and her belief that in paying five guineas in cash for her Richard Newson has legitimised their relationship. Hardy never intended the wife-sale to seem natural or even probable, although he assembled in his Commonplace Book factual accounts of such occurrences from the *Dorset County Chronicle* and the *Brighton Gazette*. The auction is clearly an extraordinary event, which violates the moral sense of the Caster-bridge community when it is discovered twenty years later. But there is a sense in which Hardy recognised the psychological temptation of such a sale, the male longing to exercise his property rights over women, to free himself from their burden with virile decision, to simplify his own conflicts by reducing them to "the ruin of good men by bad wives" (chap. 1).

This element in the novel could never have been articulated by Hardy's Victorian readers, but it has been most spiritedly expressed in our century by Irving Howe:

> To shake loose from one's wife; to discard that drooping rag of a woman, with her mute complaints and maddening passivity; to escape not by a slinking abandonment but through the public sale of her body to a stranger, as horses are sold at a fair; and thus to wrest, through sheer amoral willfulness, a second chance out of life—it is with this stroke, so insidiously attractive to male fantasy, that *The Mayor of Casterbridge* begins.
>
> (*Thomas Hardy*)

The scene, Howe goes on, speaks to "the depths of common fantasy, it summons blocked desires and transforms us into secret sharers. No matter what judgments one may make of Henchard's conduct, it is hard, after the first chapter, simply to abandon him; for through his boldness we have been drawn into complicity with the forbidden."

Howe brings an enthusiasm and an authority to his exposition of Henchard's motives that sweeps us along, although we need to be aware both that he invents a prehistory for the novel that Hardy withholds, and that in speaking of "our" common fantasies, he quietly transforms the novel into a male document. A woman's experience of this scene must be very different; indeed, there were many sensation novels of the 1870s and 1880s which presented the sale of women into marriage from the point of view of the bought wife. In Howe's reading, Hardy's novel becomes a kind of sensation-fiction, playing on the suppressed longings of its male audience, evoking sympathy for Henchard because of his crime, and not in spite of it.

In this exclusive concentration on the sale of the wife, however, Howe, like most of Hardy's critics, overlooks the simultaneous event which more profoundly determines Henchard's fate: the sale of the child. Paternity is a central subject of the book, far more important than conjugal love. Perhaps one reason why the sale of the child has been so consistently ignored by generations of Hardy critics is that the child is female. For Henchard to sell his son would be so drastic a violation of patriarchal culture that it would wrench the entire novel out of shape; but the sale of a daughter—in this case only a "tiny girl" —seems almost natural. There may even be a suggestion that this too is an act insidiously attractive to male fantasy, the rejection of the wife who has only borne female offspring.

It is the combined, premeditated sale of wife and child which launches Henchard into his second chance. Orphaned, divorced, without mother or sisters, wife or daughter, he has effectively severed all his bonds with the community of women, and reenters society alone—the new Adam, reborn, self-created, unencumbered, journeying southward without pause until he reaches Casterbridge. Henchard commits his life entirely to the male community, defining his human relationships by the male codes of money, paternity, honour, and legal contract. By his act Henchard sells out or divorces his own "feminine" self, his own need for passion, tenderness, and loyalty. The return of Susan and Elizabeth-Jane which precipitates the main phase of the novel is indeed a return of the repressed, which forces Henchard gradually to confront the tragic inadequacy of his codes, the arid limits of patriarchal power. The fantasy that women hold men back, drag them down, drain their energy, divert their strength, is nowhere so bleakly rebuked as in Hardy's tale of the "man of character." Stripped of his mayor's chain, his master's authority, his father's rights, Henchard is in a sense unmanned; but it is in moving from romantic male individualism to a more complete humanity that he becomes capable of tragic experience. Thus sex-role patterns and tragic patterns in the novel connect.

According to Christine Winfield's study of the manuscript of *The Mayor of Casterbridge,* Hardy made extensive revisions in chapter 1. The most striking detail of the early drafts was that the Henchard family was originally composed of two daughters, the elder of whom was old enough to try to dissuade Susan from going along with the sale: " 'Don't mother!' whispered the girl who sat on the woman's side. 'Father don't know what he's saying.' " On being sold to the sailor Newson, however, Susan takes the younger girl ("her favourite one") with her; Henchard keeps the other. Hardy apparently took this detail from the notice of a wife-sale in the *Brighton Gazette* for May 25, 1826: "We understand they were country people, and that the woman has had two children by her husband, one of whom he consents to keep, and the other he throws in as a makeweight to the bargain."

Hardy quickly discarded this cruel opening, and in the final text he emphasises the presence and the sale of a single infant daughter. From the beginning, she and her mother form an intimate unit, as close to each other as Henchard and his wife are separate. Susan speaks not to her husband, but to her baby, who babbles in reply; her face becomes alive when she talks to the girl. In a psychoanalytic study of Hardy, Charles K. Hofling has taken this bond between mother and daughter as the source of Henchard's jealous estrangement, but all the signs in the text point to Henchard's dissociation from the family as his own choice. The personalities of husband and wife are evidenced in all the nuances of this scene, one which they will both obsessively recall and relive. Hardy takes pains to show us Henchard's rigid unapproach-ability, his body-language eloquent of rejection. In Henchard's very footsteps there is a "dogged and cynical indifference personal to himself"; he avoids Susan's eyes and possible conversation by "reading, or pretending to read" a ballad sheet, which he must hold awkwardly with the hand thrust through the strap of his basket. The scene is in marked contrast to Mrs. Gaskell's opening in *Mary Barton,* for example, where fathers and brothers help to carry the infants; Hardy plays consciously against the reader's expectation of affectionate closeness. When Susan and Elizabeth-Jane retrace the journey many years later, they are holding hands, "the act of simple affection" (chap. 3).

Henchard's refusal of his family antedates the passionate declaration of the auction, and it is important to note that such a sale has been premeditated or at least discussed between husband and wife. There are several references to previous threats: "On a previous occasion when he had declared during a fuddle that he would dispose of her as he had done, she had replied that she would not hear him say that many times more before it happened, in the resigned tones of a fatalist " (chap. 2). When Newson asks whether Susan is willing to go with him, Henchard answers for her: "She is willing, provided she can have the child. She said so only the other day when I talked o't!" (chap. 1). After the sale, Henchard tries to evade the full responsibility for his act by blaming it on an evening's drunkenness, a temporary breakdown in reason and control; he even blames his lost wife's "simplicity" for allowing him to go through with the act: "Seize her, why didn't she know better than bring me into this disgrace! . . . She wasn't queer if I was. 'Tis like Susan to show such idiotic simplicity" (chap. 2, ellipsis mine). His anger and humiliation, none the less, cannot undo the fact that the bargain that was struck, and the "goods" that were divided (Susan takes the girl, Henchard the tools) had been long contemplated. When it is too late, Henchard chiefly regrets his over-hasty division of property: "She'd no business to take the maid—'tis my maid; and if it were the doing again she shouldn't have her!" (chap. 1).

In later scenes, Hardy gives Henchard more elaborated motives for the sale: contempt for Susan's ignorance and naiveté; and, as Henchard recalls on his first pilgrimage to Weydon-Priors, twenty-five years after the fair, his "cursed pride and mortification at being poor" (chap. 44). Financial success, in the mythology of Victorian manliness, requires the subjugation of competing passions. If it is marriage that has threatened the youthful Henchard with "the extinction of his energies" (chap. 1) a chaste life will rekindle them. Henchard's public auction and his private oath of temperance are thus consecutive stages of the same rite of passage. Henchard's oath is both an atonement for his drunken surrender to his fantasies, and a bargain with success. In Rudyard Kipling's *The Man Who Would Be King* (1899), a similar "contrack" is made, whereby Peachey Carnehan and Daniel Dravot swear to abjure liquor and women. When Dravot breaks his promise, they are exiled from their kingdom; so too will Henchard be expelled from Casterbridge when he breaks his vows. Save for the romance with Lucetta, in which he appears to play a passive role, Henchard is chaste during his long separation from his wife; he enjoys the local legend he has created of himself as the "celebrated abstaining worthy" (chap. 5); the man whose "haughty indifference to the society of woman-kind, his silent avoidance of converse with the sex" (chap. 13) is well known. His prominence in Casterbridge is produced by the commer-cialised energies of sexual sublimation, and he boasts to Farfrae that "being by nature something of a woman-hater, I have found it no hardship to keep mostly at a distance from the sex" (chap. 12). There is nothing in Henchard's consciousness which corresponds to the aching melancholy of Hardy's poem "He abjures love" (1883):

> At last I put off love,
> For twice ten years
> The daysman of my thought,
> And hope, and doing.

Indeed, in marrying Susan for the second time, Henchard forfeits something of his personal magic, and begins to lose power in the eyes of the townspeople; it is whispered that he has been "captured and enervated by the genteel widow" (chap. 13).

Henchard's emotional life is difficult to define; in the first half of the novel, Hardy gives us few direct glimpses of his psyche, and soberly refrains from the kind of romantic symbolism employed as psychological notation by the Brontës and by Dickens—dreams, doubles, hallucin-atory illnesses. But the very absence of emotion, the "void" which Hardy mentions, suggests that Henchard has divorced himself from feeling, and that it is feeling itself which obstinately retreats from him as he doggedly pursues it. When J. Hillis Miller describes Henchard as a man "driven by a passionate desire for full possession of some other person" and calls the novel "a nightmare of frustrated desire," he mis-leadingly suggests that the nature and intensity of Henchard's need is sexual. It is an absence of feeling which Henchard looks to others to supply, a craving unfocused loneliness rather than a desire towards another person. Henchard does not seek possession in the sense that he desires the confidence of others; such reciprocity as he requires, he coerces. What he wants is a "greedy exclusiveness" (chap. 41), a title; and this feeling is stimulated by male competition.

Given Henchard's misogyny, we cannot be surprised to see that his deepest feelings are reserved for another man, a surrogate brother with whom he quickly contracts a business relationship that has the emotional overtones of a marriage. Henchard thinks of giving Farfrae a third share in his business to compel him to stay; he urges that they should share a house and meals. Elizabeth-Jane is the frequent observer of the manly friendship between Henchard and Farfrae, which she idealises:

> She looked from the window and saw Henchard and Farfrae in the hay-yard talking, with that impetuous cordiality on the Mayor's part, and genial modesty on the younger man's, that was now so generally observable in their intercourse. Friendship between man and man; what a rugged strength there was in it, as evinced by these two.
>
> (chap. 15)

Yet Elizabeth-Jane is also an "accurate observer" who sees that Henchard's "tigerish affection. . . now and then resulted in a tendency to domineer" (chap. 14). It is a tigerish affection that does not respect that other's separateness, that sets its own terms of love and hate. Farfrae's passivity in this relationship is feminine at first, when he is constrained by his economic dependence on Henchard. There is nothing homosexual in their intimacy; but there is certainly on Henchard's side an open, and, he later feels, incautious embrace of homosocial friendship, an insistent male bonding. Success, for Henchard, precludes relationships with women; male cameraderie and, later, contests of manliness must take their place. He precipitately confides in Farfrae, telling him all the secrets of his past, at a point when he is determined to withhold this information from Elizabeth-Jane: "I am not going to let her know the truth" (chap. 12). Despite Henchard's sincerity, the one-sidedness of the exchange, his indifference to Farfrae's feelings if he can have his company, leads the younger man to experience their closeness as artificial, and to resist "the pressure of mechanized friendship" (chap. 16).

The community of Casterbridge itself has affinities with its Mayor when it is first infiltrated by Farfrae and the women. Like Henchard, it pulls itself in, refuses contact with its surroundings. "It is huddled all together," remarks Elizabeth-Jane when she sees it for the first time. The narrator goes on: "Its squareness was, indeed, the characteristic which most struck the eye in this antiquated borough. . . at that time, recent as it was, untouched by the faintest sprinkle of modernism. It was compact as a box of dominoes. It had no suburbs—in the ordinary sense. Country and town met at a mathematical line" (chap. 4). The

"rectangular frame" of the town recalls Hardy's descriptions of the
perpendicularity of Henchard's face; entering Casterbridge Susan and
Elizabeth-Jane encounter the "stockade of gnarled trees," the town wall,
part of its "ancient defences," the "grizzled church" whose bell tolls the
curfew with a "peremptory clang" (chap. 4). All these details suggest
Henchard, who is barricaded, authoritarian, coercive. He has become, as
Christopher Coney tells the women, "a pillar of the town" (chap. 5).

Deeply defended against intimacy and converse with women,
Henchard is vulnerable only when he has been symbolically unmanned by a fit of illness and depression; his susceptibility to these
emotional cycles (the more integrated Farfrae is immune to them) is
evidence of his divided consciousness. His romance with Lucetta takes
place during such an episode: "In my illness I sank into one of those
gloomy fits I sometimes suffer from, on account o' the loneliness of
my domestic life, when the world seems to have the blackness of hell,
and, like Job, I could curse the day that gave me birth" (chap. 12).
Again, when Henchard is living with Jopp, and becomes ill, Elizabeth-
Jane is able to penetrate his solitude, and reach his affections. At these
moments, his proud independence is overwhelmed by the woman's
warmth; he is forced into an emotionally receptive passivity. Yet
affection given in such circumstances humiliates him; he needs to demand or even coerce affection in order to feel manly and esteemed.

In health, Henchard determines the conditions of his relationships
to women with minimal attention to their feelings. His remarriage to
Susan is the product of "strict mechanical rightness" (chap. 13); his
effort to substantiate the union, to give it the appearance of some deeper emotion, is typical of his withholding of self:

> Lest she should pine for deeper affection than he could give
> he made a point of showing some semblance of it in external
> action. Among other things he had the iron railings, that
> had smiled sadly in dull rust for the last eighty years, painted
> a bright green, and the heavily-barred, small-paned Geor-
> gian sash windows enlivened with three coats of white. He
> was as kind to her as a man, mayor, and churchwarden
> could possibly be.
>
> (chap. 14)

To Susan, his kindness is an official function, and although he promises
her that he will earn his forgiveness by his future works, Henchard's
behaviour to women continues to be manipulative and proprietary. He

deceives Elizabeth-Jane in the uncomfortable masquerade of the second courtship; he has not sufficient respect for Susan to follow her instructions on the letter about her daughter's true parentage. When he wants Lucetta to marry him, he threatens to blackmail her; when he wants to get rid of Elizabeth-Jane he makes her a small allowance. He trades in women, with dictatorial letters to Farfrae, and lies to Newson, with an ego that is alive only to its own excited claims.

Having established Henchard's character in this way, Hardy introduces an overlapping series of incidents in the second half of the novel which reverses and negates the pattern of manly power and self-possession. These incidents become inexorable stages in Henchard's unmanning, forcing him to acknowledge his own human dependency and to discover his own suppressed or estranged capacity to love. The first of these episodes is the reappearance of the furmity-woman at Petty Sessions, and her public denunciation of Henchard. Placed centrally in the novel (in chapter 28), this encounter seems at first reading to have the arbitrary and fatal timing of myth; the furmity-woman simply appears in Casterbridge to commit her "nuisance" and to be arraigned. But the scene in fact follows Henchard's merciless coercion of Lucetta into a marriage she no longer desires. This violation, carried out from rivalry with Farfrae rather than disappointed love, repeats his older act of aggression against human feeling. Thus the declaration of the furmity-woman, the public humbling of Henchard by a woman, seems appropriate. It is for drunk and disorderly behaviour, for disrespect to the church and for profanity that she is accused; and her revelation of Henchard's greater disorder is an effective challenge to the authority of patriarchal law. Hardy's narrative underlines the scene explicitly as forming the "edge or turn in the incline of Henchard's fortunes. On that day—almost at that minute—he passed the ridge of prosperity and honour, and began to descend rapidly on the other side. It was strange how soon he sank in esteem. Socially he had received a startling fillip downwards; and, having already lost commercial buoyancy from rash transactions, the velocity of his descent in both aspects became accelerated every hour" (chap. 31). The emphasis at this point is very much on Henchard's fortunes and his bankruptcy; although the furmity-woman's story spreads so fast that within twenty-four hours everyone in Casterbridge knows what happened at Weydon-Priors fair, the one person from whom Henchard has most assiduously kept the secret—Elizabeth-Jane—unaccountably fails to confront him with it. Indeed, Hardy seems to have forgotten to show her reaction; when she seeks him out it is only to forgive his harshness to her. Retribution for the auction thus comes as a public rather than a private shaming; and Henchard responds publicly with his dignified withdrawal as magistrate, and later, his generous performance in bankruptcy.

The next phase of Henchard's unmanning moves into the private sphere. Hearing of Lucetta's marriage to Farfrae, he puts his former threat of blackmail into action, tormenting her by reading her letters to her husband. Henchard cannot actually bring himself to reveal her name, to cold-bloodedly destroy her happiness; but Lucetta, investing him with a more implacable will than he possesses, determines to dissuade him, and so arranges a secret morning meeting at the Roman amphitheatre, which is far more successful than even she had dared to hope:

> Her figure in the midst of the huge enclosure, the unusual plainness of her dress, her attitude of hope and appeal, so strongly revived in his soul the memory of another ill-used woman who had stood there and thus in bygone days, had now passed away into her rest, that he was unmanned, and his breast smote him for having attempted reprisals on one of a sex so weak.
>
> (chap. 35)

"Unmanning" here carries the significance of enervation, of a failure of nerve and resolve; and also the intimation of sympathy with the woman's position. The scene is carefully constructed to repeat the earlier meeting in the arena, when the wronged Susan came to Henchard in all her weakness; Henchard's "old feeling of supercilious pity for womankind in general was intensified by this suppliant appearing here as the double of the first" (chap. 35). But Hardy does not allow us such simple sentiments; he intensifies the ironic complexities that make this meeting different. There is certainly a sense in which Lucetta is both touchingly reckless of her reputation, and weak in her womanhood; these elements will come together in the fatal outcome of the skimmington-ride, when her wrecked honour and her miscarriage provide the emotional and physical shocks that kill her. While the Victorian belief in the delicacy of pregnant women, and also the statistical realities of the maternal death rate, are behind this incident (no contemporary reader of *The Mayor of Casterbridge* found it difficult to believe), Hardy obviously intends it symbolically as a demonstration of female vulnerability.

But, in another sense, Henchard is still deceiving himself about women's weakness, and flattering himself about men's strength; his "supercilious pity" for womankind is obtuse and misplaced. Lucetta's pathetic appearance, her plea of loss of attractiveness, is deliberately and desperately calculated to win his pity and to pacify his competitiveness. She is employing "the only practicable weapon left her as a woman" in this meeting with her enemy. She makes her toilette with the intention of making herself look plain; having missed a night's sleep, and being pregnant ("a natural reason for her slightly drawn look") she manages to look prematurely aged. Skilled at self-production and self-promotion, Lucetta thus turns her hand successfully to this negative strategy, with the result that Henchard ceases to find her desirable, and "no longer envied Farfrae his bargain." She has transformed herself into a drooping rag; and Henchard is again eager to get away. Lucetta's cleverest stroke is to remove the stimulus to Henchard's sense of rivalry by telling him that "neither my husband nor any other man will regard me with interest long." Although he is defeated by a woman, Henchard's understanding of women is still constituted by a kind of patriarchal innocence; he is ashamed of himself but for all the wrong reasons.

It is out of this unmanning, out of his disturbed self-esteem which has been deprived of an enemy, that Henchard tries to reassert his legitimate authority, and rebuild his diminished stature, by invading the welcoming ceremonies for the Royal Personage. Defiantly clad in "the fretted and weather-beaten garments of bygone years," Henchard indeed stands out upon the occasion, and makes himself as prominent and distinctive as Farfrae, who wears "the official gold chain with great square links, like that round the Royal unicorn" (chap. 37). The scene is the necessary preamble to the fight between the two men; Henchard's flag-waving salute to Royalty is really a challenge to Farfrae, the lion against the unicorn. He puts himself in the young mayor's path precisely in order to be snubbed and driven back, to be inflamed so that he can take his revenge in "the heat of action." The wrestling-match with Farfrae is the central male contest of the novel —rivalries over business and women resolved by hand-to-hand combat. But in mastering Farfrae, even with one hand tied behind his back, Henchard is again paradoxically unmanned, shamed, and enervated. The sense of Farfrae's indifference to him, the younger man's resistance to even this ultimate and violent coercion of passion, robs Henchard of the thrill of his victory. Again, it is the apparently weaker antagonist who prevails; and in the emotional crisis, roles are reversed so that Farfrae is the winner. As for Henchard,

> The scenes of his first acquaintance with Farfrae rushed
> back upon him—that time when the curious mixture of
> romance and thrift in the young man's composition so com-
> manded his heart that Farfrae could play upon him as on an
> instrument. So thoroughly subdued was he that he re-
> mained on the sacks in a crouching attitude, unusual for a
> man, and for such a man. Its womanliness sat tragically on
> the figure of so stern a piece of virility.
>
> (chap. 38)

The rugged friendship between man and man, so impressive when
seen from a distance by Elizabeth-Jane, comes down to this regressive,
almost foetal, scene in the loft. Henchard has finally crossed over psy-
chically and strategically to the long-repressed "feminine" side of
himself—has declared love for the first time to another person, and
accepted the meaning of that victory of the weak over the strong.
Thus, as Dale Kramer points out, "In relation to the pattern of tragedy,
the 'feminine' Henchard is by his own definition a weakened man."
But again, Henchard's surrender opens him for the first time to an understanding of human need measured in terms of feeling rather than
property. In his hasty and desperate lie to Newson, Henchard reveals
finally how dependent he has become on ties of love.

Thus the effigy which Henchard sees floating in Ten Hatches
Hole, whence he has fled in suicidal despair after the encounter with
Newson, is in fact the symbolic shell of a discarded male self, like a
chrysalis. It is the completion of his unmanning—a casting-off of the
attitudes, the empty garments, the facades of dominance and authority, now perceived by the quiet eye of Elizabeth-Jane to be no more
than "a bundle of old clothes" (chap. 41). Returning home, Henchard
is at last able to give up the tattered and defiant garments of his "primal
days," to put on clean linen. Dedicating himself to the love and protection of Elizabeth-Jane, he is humanly reborn.

The final section of the novel fulfils the implications of Henchard's
unmanning in a series of scenes which are reversals of scenes in the first
part of the book. It is Elizabeth-Jane who assumes ascendancy: "In going
and coming, in buying and selling, her word was law" (chap. 42). He
makes her tea with "housewifely care" (chap. 41). As the "netted lion"
(chap. 42), Henchard is forced into psychological indirection, to feminine
psychological manoeuvres, because he does not dare to risk a confrontation: "He would often weigh and consider for hours together the

meaning of such and such a deed or phrase of hers, when a blunt settling question would formerly have been his first instinct'' (chap. 42). It is a humbling, and yet educative and ennobling apprenticeship in human sensitivity, a dependence, Hardy writes, into which he had "declined (or, in another sense, to which he had advanced)" (chap. 42).

In his final self-imposed exile, Henchard carries with him mementos of Elizabeth-Jane: "gloves, shoes, a scrap of her handwriting,...a curl of her hair" (chap. 44, ellipsis mine). Retracing his past, he has chosen to burden himself with reminders of womanhood, and to plot his journey in relation to a female centre. Even the circle he traces around the "centripetal influence" (chap. 44) of his stepdaughter contrasts with the defended squareness of the Casterbridge he has left behind, the straight grain of masculine direction. Henchard's final pilgrimage, to Elizabeth-Jane's wedding, is, detail by detail, a reliving of the journey made by the women at the beginning of the novel. He enters the town for the last time as they entered at the first: the poor relation, the suppliant, the outsider. "As a Samson shorn" (chap. 44) he timidly presents himself at the kitchen-door, and from the empty back-parlour awaits Elizabeth-Jane's arrival. As Susan and Elizabeth-Jane watched him preside over the meeting of the Council, so he now must watch his stepdaughter preside over her wedding-party. As Susan was overpowered by the sight of her former husband's glory, and wished only "to go—pass away—die" (chap. 5), so is Henchard shamed and overwhelmed by Elizabeth-Jane's moral ascendancy. What is threatened and forgotten in the first instance comes to pass in the second—the rejected guest departs, and neither Elizabeth-Jane nor the reader sees him more.

In a sense which Hardy fully allows, the moral as well as the temporal victory of the novel is Elizabeth-Jane's. It is she to whom the concluding paragraphs are given, with their message of domestic serenity, their Victorian feminine wisdom of "making limited opportunities endurable," albeit in "a general drama of pain" (chap. 45). Casterbridge, under the combined leadership of Elizabeth-Jane and Farfrae, is a gentled community, its old rough ways made civil, its rough edges softened. We might read the story of Henchard as a tragic taming of the heroic will, the bending and breaking of his savage male defiance in contest with a stoic female endurance. In such a reading, Henchard becomes a second Heathcliff, who is also overcome by the domestic power of a daughter-figure; like Heathcliff, Henchard is subdued first to the placidities of the grange, then to the grave.

Yet this romantic and nostalgic reading would underestimate Hardy's generosity of imagination. Virginia Woolf, one of Hardy's earliest feminist critics, attributed the "tragic power" of his characters to "a force within them which cannot be defined, a force of love or of hate, a force which in the men is the cause of rebellion against life, and in the women implies an illimitable capacity for suffering." In Henchard the forces of male rebellion and female suffering ultimately conjoin; and in this unmanning Hardy achieves a tragic power unequalled in Victorian fiction. It may indeed be true that Hardy could not be accounted a feminist in the political terms of the 1880s, or the 1970s; but in *The Mayor of Casterbridge* the feminist critic can see Hardy's swerving from the bluff virility of the Rabelais Club, and the misogyny of Gosse, towards his own insistent and original exploration of human motivation. The skills which Henchard struggles finally to learn, skills of observation, attention, sensitivity, and compassion, are also those of the novelist; and they are feminine perhaps, if one contrasts them to the skills of the architect or the statesman. But it is because Hardy dares so fully to acknowledge this side of his own art, to pursue the feminine spirit in his man of character, that his hero, like the great heroines he would create in the 1890s, is more Shakespearean than Victorian.

Thomas Hardy's
The Mayor of Casterbridge:
Reversing the Real

George Levine

> *I like a story with a bad moral. My sonnies, all true stories have a coarseness or a bad moral, depend upon't. If the story tellers could have got decency and good morals from true stories, who'd ha' troubled to invent parables?*
>
> REUBEN DEWY, in *Under the Greenwood Tree*

Reuben Dewy seems a comic apologist for the later Hardy, in whose novels we find stunning reversals of the emphases and assumptions that guided realists through the first half of the nineteenth century. For Hardy, whose reserved hostility to the arbitrariness and cruelty of most social conventions is well known, the fullest truth inheres not in the moral ideals of modern civilization but in the essential passions and energies of human nature. These may be detected most convincingly in the unselfconscious traditions of societies, close, in their rhythms and morals, to the processes of nature, in which sporadic violence is a norm, and only barely touched by the movements of history. Or, more interestingly, the energies are most vividly present in those characters who have, for whatever reason, been touched into at least a primitive consciousness of the constrictions imposed by tradition, by social expectations, by moral ideals. The emphasis in Hardy shifts, not so much from the "ordinary," as from the realist's conception of ordinariness. His protagonists, from Dick Dewy to Michael Henchard, are all, in some respects, quite ordinary; yet they increasingly become

---

From *The Realistic Imagination: English Fiction from* Frankenstein *to* Lady Chatterley. ©1981 by the University of Chicago. University of Chicago Press, 1981.

focuses of tragic intensity. Their desires are not the romantic dreams to be mocked and minimized by wise or ironic narrators, but the stuff of nature and of tragedy.

In Hardy's fiction the realist's acceptance of compromise becomes itself a social convention, or an ideal either deadening when it is pursued without consciousness of the pain of experience, or almost unattainable but by hard discipline. The disenchanted acceptance of the ordinary and decent in the sharp sunlight that banishes the fantasies of romance; the recognition of the needs of others and of the limitations of the self; the revelation like Gwendolen Harleth's, that "her horizon was but a dipping onward of an existence with which her own was revolving"; the discovery of one's own mixed nature, of the flaws in one's lover, of the insuperable pressures of society—all of these normal consequences of the realities of Victorian fiction become in Hardy not less inevitable, but less a means to moral growth, and less adequate as a summary of reality. They become, rather, almost unendurable occasions for the tragic. Hardy's fiction gives the impression that, although the narrator does what he can to minimize them, the stakes have been raised, not only far beyond the Trollopian norm, but to the level of the absolute. There are, to be sure, characters in his novels who make the compromise, but the focus is on a prior reality. Hardy's protagonists seem to echo the experience of Victor Frankenstein, whose history is a sequence of waverings between an absolute ideal and a domestic compromise. One feels, retrospectively, a Hardyesque quality to Frankenstein's last uncompromising recovery of his dream amid the vision of failures and compromises: "Yet another may succeed."

Indeed, in Hardy, the compromise with the dream of large romantic aspiration has itself something of the quality of romantic dream about it. That is, such compromise is intrinsically unavailable to the instinctively aspiring protagonists who, like Frankenstein, are impelled not by any moral consideration it may at any moment rationally offer, but by a longing for the absolute and for the pure power of the self triumphant. If *Under the Greenwood Tree* ends with one of those ironically imagined compromises, as a comedy, it nevertheless has within it the elements that will later make for tragedy. And it points forward, beyond its own pages, with a pleasant and satisfying humor that belies the seriousness of the possibilities: " 'O, 'tis the nightingale,' murmured she, and thought of a secret she should never tell" (chap. 5).

In later work, the attempt to limit aspiration is clearly a dream. When, in *The Woodlanders,* Dr. Edred Fitzpiers, in his Lydgatian retreat to a country practice, contemplates marrying Grace Melbury and set-tling in Little Hintock, he asks himself: "Why should he go further into the world than where he was? The secret of happiness lay in limit-ing the aspirations; these men's thoughts were coterminous with the margin of the Hintock woodlands, and why should not his be likewise limited—a small practice among the people around him being the bound of his desires." What might in an earlier novel have been the disenchanted revelation of the inevitability and virtue of limits is for Fitzpiers an untenable dream. Immediately after he does in fact marry Grace, he falls in love with the richer and more "modern" Mrs. Charmond. The men whose thoughts were "coterminous" with the woods are them-selves a dying breed, and the volatile and unstable Fitzpiers, who sim-ply cannot internalize the limits he almost chooses, though he is an anomaly at Hintock represents a majority of the culture at large. The strangely distant narrator knows this, although none of his characters does. Fitzpiers, to be sure, is too shallow to be regarded as Pro-methean; yet the very compromises he is forced to make at the end of the novel in returning to Grace diminish him, as Grace's return to him leaves us only with the dignity of Marty South, who has been able to remain true to her impossible ideal. The novel implies no growth in compromise, only loss of the little dignity Fitzpiers had in the authen-ticity of his passion.

Thus if Hardy endorses the notion that the "secret of happiness lay in limiting the aspiration," it does not mean that he found the idea attractive or even practicable. Happiness is not a normal or safe human condition. The characters who aspire absurdly and beyond the control of their own will have about them a quality of heroism that distin-guishes them impressively from those less ambitious and more con-trolled, those who have not tested the limits of social constriction or aspired beyond the security of their station. Hardy's narrative voice keeps him aloofly distant from the passions it describes; he remains almost archaeologically disengaged from the action, protected from it so thoroughly that he can afford to release within his narratives pre-cisely those energies that earlier realists, in their compassionate focus on the details and surfaces of ordinary experience, kept submerged. The self-effacement of the "Everlasting Yea," which might be taken as the ideology of the Victorian realist's world, is not in Hardy a tough-minded acceptance of a limiting reality. Rather, it is an act of self-protection, felt in the narrator's own refusal to engage himself, and yet largely and tragically inaccessible to the actors in his dramas. It is unnatural in life, requiring extraordinary discipline of will and feeling, and probably unsustainable. Self-denial is itself a romantic dream, and its consequences can be as destructive.

The primary reality among Hardy's characters is their uncontrollable, irrational desire in an imperfect world. The large aspirations that mark the romantic hero, that are manifested in Victor Frankenstein with catastrophic and Tertius Lydgate with pathetic results are not, for Hardy, rare exceptions to the human norm. They can manifest themselves anywhere; they can be felt, in small, in Dick Dewy's love of Fancy Day, as well as in Giles Winterborne's love of Grace. Whereas realism gets much of its originating thrust from a comic and ironic view of romantic aspiration and, through parody or Thackerayan satire, denigrates it as hypocritical or silly, Hardy treats aspiration neither as an aberration nor as a falsification, but as representatively, critically, tragically human. The qualities that distinguish the human from the merely natural are intelligence and language and the capacity to imagine and desire beyond the limits of nature. The human is the only element in nature incompatible with it.

Essentially, then, Hardy saw a world that was at once continuous with yet in almost every major respect the reverse of the world projected with such moral rigor, sincerity, and toughmindedness by the Victorian realists. If his landscape, for example, excludes the Alpine peaks, for an almost loving but careful registration of the local scene, it does not exclude the intensities that normally accompany them. The violence of the natural world intrudes into the flattest landscapes; and the upland stretches of Egdon Heath, "a vast tract of unenclosed wild," the hill above Weydon-Priors where Henchard sells his wife, the height from which Jude spies the distant lights of Christminster—all these release uncontrollable energies that destroy with the force of an Alpine torrent. With the realist's particularity and with a movingly precise vision of the details and energies of the natural world, Hardy yet creates a universe that stands in almost parodic antithesis to such landscapes as those of Barchester or Loamshire, although they might be taken as literally almost identical.

It is antithetical, for one thing, in respect to the rules of civilized living, according to which Trollope so carefully organizes his world, and to the notion that civilization is both more interesting and more important than the more primitive worlds it has displaced. Civilization, his narratives demonstrate, is an arbitrarily acquired and extremely thin veneer over what is quintessentially human. The human, moreover, is both "natural" and hostile to nature, is both material and ideal. The rules of society, which govern Trollope's novels and largely determine both the texture and values of characters' lives, do not, even in Trollope, adequately cover the variety and complexity of experience; but in Hardy, those rules are powerful forces in the imagination of his characters and utterly powerless to control their actual behavior, while irrelevant to the shape of the narrative. That is, they serve as deadly obstacles to what is most valuable and interesting about humans and their fictions—the strength of desire. Notoriously, it is social convention that dooms Tess's relation to Angel Clare; it is social convention that keeps Jude from fulfilling his early ambition. Yet those conventions, mere "ideas" by which society organizes itself, are powerless to keep Jude or Tess safe from the instincts that so often govern their behavior. The conventions in Hardy exist not as a general ideal on which variations must be played but as a human fiction that is both necessary for society and destructive of its most interesting members. In effect, Hardy replaces Whately with Freud (and the Schopenhauer that lay behind Freud). The world does not correspond to human need, bringing individual and social together. But human need is divided and self-destructive, requiring both the protection of society and freedom from its restraints.

The antithesis implicit in Hardy's attitude to the rules manifests itself as well in his choice of subjects. There is, of course, a long tradition in realistic fiction of the comic use of peasants and rustics. Their lives are imagined as light echoes of the dominant narratives, which relate to less rustic, more literate protagonists. In Scott we find a world of rustics who bear with them the vitality and the authenticity of unselfconsciously transmitted tradition and who frequently have a fictional life richer than that of the aristocratic heroes and heroines. In George Eliot, rustics often appear to comment shrewdly on the blindnesses of the protagonists and to invoke traditional wisdom with choric force, so as to impose a traditional pattern on the realist's potential disaster. In Hardy, however, although the tradition of both Scott and George Eliot is at work, the focus is distributed so that rustics and protagonists often blend into each other; rustics might well be protagonists. Clym Yeobright and Grace Melbury are only two who are educated beyond their class and are variously pulled back into it. To Trollope, a focus on a Dick Dewy or a Giles Winterbourne might have seemed misguided or wasteful. Where Trollope had argued that educated classes are on the whole morally and intellectually superior, and everywhere in his fiction implied the need for and the power of civilization to repress or outstrip savagery, Hardy opposed such a view, and novels of manners, of the drawing room and of the club:

> All persons who have thoughtfully compared class with class —and the wider their experience the more pronounced their opinion—are convinced that education has as yet but little broken or modified the waves of human impulse on which deeds and words depend. So that in the portraiture of scenes in any way emotional or climactic—the highest province of fiction—the peer and peasant stand on much the same level; the woman who makes the satin train and the woman who wears it. In the lapse of countless ages, no doubt, improved systems of moral education will considerably and appreciably elevate even the involuntary instincts of human nature; but at present culture has only affected the surface of those lives with which it has come in contact, bending down the passions of those predisposed to turmoil as by a silken thread only, which the first ebullition suffices to break. With regard to what may be termed the minor key of action and speech—the unemotional every-day doings of men—social refinement operates upon character in a way which is oftener than not prejudicial to vigorous portraiture, by making the exterior of their screen rather than their index, as with untutored mankind.
>
> ("The Profitable Reading of Fiction")

On this account, realism, in its preoccupation with social rules and material surfaces, misses entirely the primary realities of human experience. Civilization is a veneer, and reality lies primarily in what realists would have thought of as extreme—in the very checkering they attempted to eschew: the emotional or climactic is the highest province of fiction.

This sort of emphasis leads away from the realist's concentration on character toward a more traditional (or romantic) emphasis on plot. Hardy's finding in tragedy a model for his narratives is a logical consequence of the new preoccupation with narrative structure. And in his own writing about fiction, he talks about the importance of structure with a seriousness exceeded only by George Eliot among the novelists who immediately preceded him. Symptomatically, as he looks back for models of satisfactorily structured novels, he singles out Scott's *Bride of Lammermoor*—"an almost perfect specimen of form." Thackeray's disapproval of that novel, as I suggested [elsewhere], had to do with its very singularity among Scott's works. All of Hardy's critical and narrative instincts opposed Thackeray's casualness about narrative form. Like George Eliot, instead, he asks that the work of art have the structure of an "organism," and that everything in it be related to everything else.

In some well-known notes on fiction Hardy laid out several propositions that help clarify how, in his peculiar relation to realism, he had moved to a more "modern" preoccupation with structure. He is realism's continuator and adversary:

> The real, if unavowed, purpose of fiction is to give pleasure by gratifying the love of the uncommon in human experience, mental or corporeal.
>
> This is done all the more perfectly in proportion as the reader is illuded to believe the personages true and real like himself.
>
> Solely to this latter end a work of fiction should be a precise transcript of ordinary life: but,
>
> The uncommon would be absent and the interest lost. Hence,
>
> The writer's problem is, how to strike the balance between the uncommon and the ordinary so as on the one hand to give interest, on the other to give reality.
>
> In working out this problem, human nature must never be made abnormal, which is introducing incredibility. The uncommonness must be in the events, not in the characters; and the writer's art lies in shaping that uncommonness while disguising its unlikelihood, if it be unlikely.
>
> (Florence Emily Hardy, *The Early Life of Thomas Hardy*)

The "uncommon," the "ordinary," "transcript," "illusion"—these are by now all familiar terms or concepts, but Hardy has somehow rearranged them. He argues for the risk of incredibility in plot in order to insure credibility in character. His actual practice seems to correspond to this argument, and *The Mayor of Casterbridge,* in a mere recital of its events, would seem absurd; yet from it Henchard emerges with overwhelming conviction. The love of the "uncommon" that Hardy attributes to his readers is, surely, his own love; and the "ordinary" world as he imagines it is a world of intensities and extremes. "Romanticism," he had written a few months earlier, "will exist in human nature as long as human nature itself exists."

These notes indicate what is evident in the fictions, that as a self-conscious artist, Hardy was profoundly aware of the fact that art was—and ought to be—something other than reality. He seeks for organism and relevance in his fictions, for the symmetry of plot, for the imposition of consciousness upon experience. And in this respect, he is radically, at least in intention, at odds with all the realists who preceded him. He develops to an extreme their sense that experience and history may, in the long run, be without meaning or value. That sense allowed Thackeray to risk the near dissolution of many of his later narratives. It forced George Eliot to a new imagination of narrative. But for Hardy it is precisely the disorder of experience that requires the order of art. Value is human; it does not inhere in nature. If as Henry James and J. Hillis Miller have argued, the novelist's model is the historian, Hardy's model is self-consciously the artist. For, he says, "History is rather a stream than a tree. There is nothing organic in its shape, nothing systematic in its development. It flows on like a thunderstorm-rill by the road side; now a straw turns it this way, now a tiny barrier of sand that." Hardy's is the world of Huxley's *Evolution and Ethics,* a world in which not following nature but building human structures against it is the way to survival. For Hardy, art is the place where structures can be created against the disorders and irrelevances of history. For art unabashedly projects consciousness upon raw experience, upon "crass casualty." Art, indeed, names that.

It is this special aesthetic quality that we find in all of his great novels; an unembarrassed symmetry of action and reaction imposed upon the inorganic streaming of experience. The novelist hides behind his language and peeks out into the wilderness, even the savagery, that contends in human nature with the constructed ideals of society. Hardy shares with Thackeray the realist's sense of how every climax becomes only a moment in a process; and thus of how the dream of a stable achievement, of closure, is misguided in all respects but that of death. "It is the on-going—*i.e.* the 'becoming' of the world that produces its sadness," says Hardy. "If the world stood still at a felicitous moment there would be no sadness in it." Yet unlike Thackeray, who retreats into the guise of the sage old disenchanted figure whose narrative strategy is to deflate each climactic moment as it comes, Hardy moves even further from the action in his distinctively labored and distant voice and yet produces dramas of desire and will, focusing on moments of passion with tragic clarity and intensity.

Thus realism, as practiced by Trollope or advocated by the early George Eliot, seemed to Hardy merely conventional—as conventional, at least, as Austen perceived the Gothic novel to be. "Representations" of reality were of necessity merely conventions of ways to imagine reality. The disparity between art (organic) and life (merely streaming) assured that Hardy's own carefully outlined structures were no less "true" than the large loose monsters of the other Victorians. In the curious progress of realism's self-contradictory impulses, Hardy can be taken as the perfect exemplar. His fiction almost defines itself as being what Trollope's and Thackeray's is not, and all in the name of a faithful and sincere registration of the way things are. The way things are had changed, so that Hardy might have subscribed to the credos of realism . . . although he constantly violated its conventions. The world had been transformed, and what the "dull grey eyes," the "cold lentils" actually indicated could not be contained within the dominant modes of mid-century realism. Hardy was essentially concerned with the artist's responsibility to this new imagination of the world:

> By a sincere school of Fiction we may understand a Fiction that expresses truly the views of life prevalent in its time, by means of a selected chain of action best suited for their exhibition. What are the prevalent views of life just now is a question upon which it is not necessary to enter further than to suggest that the most natural method of presenting them, the method most in accordance with the views themselves, seems to be by a procedure mainly impassive in its tone and tragic in its developments.
>
> ("Candour in English Fiction")

The special pleading here is obvious. Yet it is true that the dominant comic mode of the realist tradition, evident from Jane Austen to mid-century, was shifting even in Trollope, but certainly in George Eliot. Comic endings had become more questionable—not only in Thackeray's *Newcomes,* or in *Little Dorrit,* but even in such Trollopian comedies as *Mr. Scarborough's Family,* or in *Middlemarch;* and catastrophe became a possible conclusion—in *The Mill on the Floss,* or *Beauchamp's Career.* The "impassivity" Hardy advocates suggests something of the defensive maneuvering required of his narrators, whose voices imply the discovery that the limiting of aspirations is not a morally healthy repression of precivilized human energy, but directly contrary to the human condition. Such repression cannot end in comic compromise, but only in violent explosions of unaccountable and catastrophic energy.

But advancing secularism and an exciting yet disruptive new

science had in fact radically transformed "the view of life prevalent" in Hardy's time. I will be discussing this transformation in the following chapters on George Eliot and Conrad, whose response to it seems, finally, even more radical than Hardy's. In every case, however, this transformation had vast consequences for fiction. It entailed the final dissolution of the kind of vision that allowed Whately to endorse Austen's realism by in effect endorsing reality, and that, in various ways, lay behind almost all Victorian realism to mid-century. Yet more important (since all the writers we have looked at had already been undercutting traditional faith in the meaning and order of the world), the transformation would ultimately disrupt the process of realism by which it moved through parody to new imaginations of the real requiring yet newer parody.

Hardy's kind of tragic and shapely—"geometric," he would call it—fiction does not follow out the full disruptive consequences of the new world view. Instead, it rebounds almost parodically away from earlier conventions of realism, while sustaining much of its mood. He had a deep commitment to the conventions of art itself rather different in kind from that of the realists, for whom art required attention more to the implications for living than to the medium itself. Thus, with all his self-consciousness about the indifference of the universe, Hardy could never imagine an antiart which, in its own dissolutions of traditional forms, mimicked the dissolution of meaning in the universe. "Good fiction," he wrote, "may be defined as the kind of imagi-native writing which lies nearest to the epic, dramatic, or narrative masterpieces of the past." In addition, Hardy's realism is distinctly continuous with Wordsworth's. Experience must, in Hardy, be made meaningful, even if the "meaning" is that the world has none, or is inimical to human consciousness. Beyond the disastrous failures of a nature ever completing itself, never complete, of a world incompatible with human intelligence, there remains the power and dignity of the human itself. Such power can *make* the world relevant by imposing on it human intelligence. Michael Henchard has more than a nominal connection to Wordsworth's Michael. In seeing through the veneer of civilization, Hardy finds a Wordsworthian universality even in the peculiarities of his peasants. As he noted in his diary, apparently in 1881: "Consider the Wordsworthian dictum (the more perfectly the natural object is reproduced, the more truly poetic the picture). This reproduction is achieved by seeing into the heart of a thing . . . and is realism, in fact, though through being pursued by means of the imagination it is confounded with invention." He could not drop at least this aspect of the realist's program although all his emphasis is on imagination, enthusiasm, passion. Realism defends him from the charge of mere invention. He is, rather, seeing with Ruskinian and Wordsworthian clarity.

But in Hardy, too, the ultimate severance of art from representation is already more than latent in his primary belief in the incompatibility of consciousness with the entirely material world from which it aberrantly emerged. As at last in *The Well-Beloved,* Hardy is continuously aware of the disparity between the human imagination of the real and the possibilities of the real itself. At its worst, this issues in what was often called Hardy's fashionable pessimism. But in the drama of the novels themselves, it points directly back to the sort of world implied in *Frankenstein,* one in which inexplicable destructive forces issued inevitably out of what might have seemed the most ideal conditions of civilization. The unnameable nonhuman reality burst forth, as he puts it, at "the first ebullition," over the impossibly tenuous restraints of civilization. In Hardy, the monster stalks freely and visibly again, bringing with him an art strikingly akin to that which the early great realist practitioners of realism, in their imagination of an unchecked world of compromise and disenchantment, had laughed away through their parodies and satires.

II

The Mayor of Casterbridge is the novel that most precisely and powerfully focuses the relation of Hardy's new vision both to the realistic tradition out of which, and against which, it is imagined, and to the tradition of romance. It is a novel that belongs centrally in the nineteenth century, echoing with its naturalistic fidelity, with its preoccupation with "character," with its thematic concern about the relation of the individual to society, about the relation between past and present; yet it is also a novel that embodies a distinctly "modern" vision and that points forward, as Albert Guerard has noted, to the work of Conrad and the early modernists. Henchard, Guerard explains, traces a career remarkably similar to that of Conrad's Lord Jim, whose life is determined by a single instinctive act which he is doomed to redeem and repeat to the end. But I consider Hardy's novel here, rather than at the end of this study, because "modern" as Hardy's fiction may seem to be, it does not follow out in its narrative method the full implications of its vision. Reversal is not a rejection of order. *The Mayor of*

Casterbridge evidences in a moving and satisfying way Hardy's fundamental unwillingness to surrender to the disorder he sees. It is a final
assertion of the possibility of human control, however monstrous,
against the ultimate horror of a world inimical to intelligence, casually
destructive, and inaccessible to the very language by which humanity
designates it. It risks the "violence" Bersani attributes to narrativity in
order to affirm the power of imagination and the necessity for order.

In the preceding chapters, I have been concerned to examine the
way realism moved toward an increasing multiplication and fragmen-
tation of narrative as writers attempted to come to terms with their
developing sense of the disorder of experience itself, and of the violence to reality done by dogma, ideals, and selfish desire. In Trollope
and Thackeray, the contrivances of fictional ordering are postponed or
diluted or, in subplots, qualified by alternatives. The large loose baggy
monster had come to represent not so much an aesthetic slovenliness as
one valid aesthetic consequence of the realistic vision, requiring us to
see any narrative line as only one possibility. The rigorous shaping
hand of the novelist, which in a different sort of art was to be hidden
under the pressure of a Flaubertian aesthetic ideal, was for the Victorians
to be restrained in the interest of the most honest possible registration
of reality. The artist, among the Victorians, might comment and judge,
but not control.

The Mayor of Casterbridge is an aggressively manipulated narrative.
It belongs, in this respect, to a narrative tradition governed not by the
criterion of plausibility but by that of coherence of feeling. It is one of
those remarkable Hardyesque achievements that manage to carry
overwhelming conviction while, at every instance, inviting us to dis-
miss them as incredible. From the perspective of realism, this represents a falsifying tradition of romance; but in *The Mayor of Casterbridge*
it is brought into uneasy but effective conjunction with the traditions
of realism. The organizing pressure of feeling that gives to romance its
distinctive form and makes both *Frankenstein* and *Wuthering Heights* so
remarkably symmetrical has an interesting and honorable life among
the Victorians. Even among them, where the three-decker novel pre-
dominated, and serial publication encouraged the very disorder the
realist instinctively found authentic, there are fictions that focus intensely around a single consciousness and absorb the world into that
consciousness's needs. We have seen [elsewhere] that even *Northanger
Abbey* is controlled by the desires (however long delayed and uncer-
tainly understood) of the heroine. Catherine Morland, in her con-

sumption of the world about her, bespeaks those monstrous energies that Austen, in creating her, was mocking. *Jane Eyre,* too, reflects the shaping of experience to personal need. And even *Great Expectations* is ultimately constructed so that almost everything in the world reflects Pip or refers to him.

These narratives, all directed—within the conventions of realism —to demonstrate the folly of great expectations and the moral disaster of imposing the self on experience, nevertheless blur the distinction between the self and other. The special strength of the narratives depends largely on the sense, beyond reason or the power of the mimetic method to record, that the protagonist's fate is somehow entirely created by the self. It is not at all simply wish fulfillment, not at all simply that Jane Eyre gets Rochester but, rather, that she gets the conditions in which she actually lives by virtue of qualities intrinsic to herself. The figure that keeps her from Rochester, "Bertha Mason," is an element of herself that she consciously restrains but cannot eliminate, so that the figure that gives her Rochester is also Bertha Mason, who literally purges Rochester of those qualities that make him unfit for Jane. The landscape of *Jane Eyre* is a romantic one in that it is the self projected, with all its irrationalities and inconsistencies. One can talk and must talk about a literal landscape and about other characters, but *Jane Eyre* is also most powerfully a novel of the self coming to terms with itself. Similarly, as Julian Moynahan brilliantly showed many years ago, the landscape of *Great Expectations* is Pip projected outward. The realist's lesson of disenchantment is there not simply a new recognition of the incompatibility of selfish aspiration with a contingent and varied universe, full of other selves, but a discovery of personal responsibility and, indeed, of personal power. Pip, in a sense, wills the destruction of his sister, of Miss Havisham, and almost of himself. Such novels, like *Frankenstein* gothically before them, reflect the power of consciousness even as they dramatize the powerlessness of the self apart from the community. Each of them projects some monster into the world as Maggie Tulliver evokes the flood, and Victor creates his hideous progeny.

In such novels, plot bears the burden of uncommonness, and in *The Mayor of Casterbridge,* Hardy is consistent with his own dictum that the unreality should be in plot rather than in "character." But plot is not merely—if it is also—a vehicle for the display of "character." It is the means through which Hardy imposes a structure on the world and animates it. One feels in the plot of *The Mayor of Casterbridge* a myster-

ious but irresistible power lying behind the beautifully observed quotidian and asserting itself against the will of the protagonist in such a
way as to imply a dramatic if uneven contest. One feels it despite the
simple and abstract assertion of Hardy's pessimism, as in the narrator's
invocation of the "ingenious machinery contrived by the Gods for
reducing human possibilities of amelioration to a minimum." However much Hardy will imply or, as in later novels, overtly argue the
indifference of the world to human concerns, the plot of *The Mayor of
Casterbridge,* the many twists, the curious and convincing hostility of
the elements, of the landscape itself, so resonant with life, imply a
meaningful—if perverse—world. And if this "plot" is further complicated by a richly subtle scene of the way the "external" animosity is
inherent in the human will itself, that insight does not diminish the force
with which the structure of the novel resists the disorder and meaning-
lessness toward which, we have seen, realism has been moving. The effect
is achieved particularly by Hardy's relish for the "uncommon," his
insistence on facing up to the most extreme possibilities.

In the almost numbing sequence of catastrophes that befall
Henchard, none is diminished or minimized. They exist not in an aura
of nostalgia for intensities no longer available to the disenchanted narrator in the grey modern world, but as continuing realities that no
wisdom can efface. Henchard, the "man of character" whose story the
subtitle announces, is imagined as precisely the sort of character who
would find the realist's disenchantment unendurable. His story is, in a
way, about Victorian realism and possible alternatives. Henchard
moves in a landscape of ancient ruins, cornfields, Egdon Heath, all
governed by the inexorable repetitions and transformations of time,
all threatening to absorb him: yet in this landscape Henchard asserts
his specialness, refusing to acquiesce in or compromise with the forces
that require that he diminish his claims and make his peace. But he
outwits both society and nature by anticipating the worst they can do,
and he leaves his "will" to assert his final contradictory power.

Against the extravagance of Henchard's plot, there is a realist's
subplot—plausible, moderate, compromised. Farfrae is a character
from a mid-Victorian novel whose moderate demands, quiet self-
interest, refusal of excess, and emotional shallowness all operate within the text as a commentary on Henchard's way of being. Farfrae's
amiable shallowness is first observed in his moving rendition of "It's
hame, and it's hame, hame fain would I be, O hame, hame, hame to my
ain countree." This is followed by his announcement that he is going

to America, and echoes with a developing realist preoccupation with dilettantism. Hardy seems to be taking up the tradition that had led Thackeray to focus on a protagonist like Pendennis, capable of surviving and of resisting the worst excesses of moral enthusiasm, by virtue of a fundamental shallowness; and in a voice reverberating with the awareness that the secret of happiness lay in the limiting of aspiration, he tests the mixed and compromised realist hero, Farfrae, against the overreacher, Henchard. When, at the end, Elizabeth-Jane attempts to enlist Farfrae in a search for the wandering Henchard, Farfrae has no objections: "Although Farfrae had never so passionately liked Henchard as Henchard had liked him, he had, on the other hand, never so passionately hated in the same direction as his former friend had done; and he was therefore not the least indisposed to assist Elizabeth-Jane in her laudable plan." It is part of the astonishing achievement of the novel that we feel in Farfrae's generosity less that is admirable than we would if, Henchard-like, he had been vengeful and adamant. Farfrae achieves the life of compromise and stands finally in the landscape of Casterbridge humanly diminished before Henchard's grand disasters. Henchard's story and Farfrae's comment almost parodically on each other. Henchard's reverses the comic pattern, which informed the earlier realistic fiction, and in its reversal averts the ultimate inconsequence of the middling life Farfrae enacts, the realist's casual disorder of experience and the inhuman indifference of Hardy's nature.

Ironically, Hardy's violation of the conventions of realism does not free his narrative for the creative unions of romance but leads to the very defeat from which, one might have thought, the rejection of realism would have protected it. Even here, Hardy plays with realism's conventions; for it was certainly a part—if an "impure" part—of the conventions of Victorian realism that manipulations of plot (Dickensian coincidences are only the extreme examples) enact for the protagonists the desires hindered by the particularities and complexities of experience. We have seen such enactment in *Northanger Abbey;* but Thackeray uses it as well, if almost cynically, and Trollope, too, with casual ease. The comic tradition of the novel relied very heavily on the coincidence, as it is used so conventionally and effectively in *Tom Jones.* But in the happy ending for Farfrae and Elizabeth-Jane, that tradition is implicitly criticized. If the realist must use coincidence to resolve narratives, the most "realistic" use of such coincidence, Hardy implies, is not comic conjunction but tragic disruption. Coincidence must become the chance that explodes the fantasy of happiness. If Elizabeth-Jane goes on to a life of "unbroken tranquility," she continues to wonder "at the persistence of the unforeseen." Everything in the novel points to the exceptional nature, not of disaster, but of that "tranquility"; what predominates in life is the "unforeseen," and injustice. Elizabeth-Jane, whose relation to the narrative is of major importance, must renounce the enthusiasm that made Henchard so much a man of character. In Elizabeth-Jane it is not shallowness, as it is with Farfrae, that makes for survival. Although she is one of the lucky ones, she *knows* she is lucky. And having had more passion to begin with, she knows the price of tranquility, as Farfrae does not.

Thus, despite Elizabeth-Jane's concluding voice, *The Mayor of Casterbridge* is almost a celebration of disaster. The disaster, or at least the willingness to confront it, is Henchard's dignity. He chooses his own disaster, down to his last moments when, with the possibility of a new beginning before him, we learn that "he had no desire." Henchard becomes an inverted romantic hero: he makes his own fate. The novel, while asserting man's contingent and compromised nature, imagines the possibility of something freer. It pushes beyond the "small solicitation of circumstance" to a celebration of demonic human energies that realism had, at least since Frankenstein, been struggling to repress.

III

Critics have long recognized that Henchard, in one way or another, *is* the world of *The Mayor of Casterbridge*. Like Frankenstein before him, he absorbs all external reality into his dream of the self. Technically, this means not only that every character and event in the novel relates directly to Henchard, but that the more intensely one examines the novel, the more evident it is that every character in it reflects aspects of his enormous selfhood. As Victor Frankenstein is his monster's double, but also Clerval's, his mother's, his brother's, Walton's, so Henchard is the double of Farfrae and Elizabeth-Jane, Jopp and Abel Whittle, Newson and Lucetta. As Victor moves with erratic repetitiveness from act to reaction, from aspiration to repentance, so Henchard enacts his self-division and Hardy projects that division on the landscape of his narrative. It is all done with the recklessness of conventional plausibility that marks Gothic conventions, and yet it achieves a new sort of plausibility. For the large techniques of romance are incorporated here into the texture of a realism that allows every monstrous quirk its credible place in a social, historical, and geographical context belonging importantly to the conventions of realism. The landscape of the self in this novel almost displaces the landscape of that hard, unaccommodating actual to the representation of which the realist has always been dedicated. But self and other exist here in a delicate balance, and it is probably more appropriate to say that in *The Mayor of Casterbridge* Hardy makes overt the continuing and inevitable presence of romance in all realistic fiction.

We may take the remarkable first scene, in which Henchard sells his wife, as a perfect example of the way Hardy's narrative embodies the tensions between the conventions of realism and that of romance in style and substance, and the way it daringly asserts the presence of the uncommon in the common. The whole sequence confronts directly the problem of inventing satisfying ways to cope with the limiting pressures of the realist's contingent world on large human energies and aspiration. Exploiting the conventions of realism to free itself from the conventional real, and at the risk both of alienating its readers by claiming kinship with great tragedy or mere sensationalism and of disrupting the life of its protagonists, Hardy's narrative implies both a new freedom of imagination and a new conception of human dignity. The freedom and the dignity are precisely in the willingness to take the risk—of uncommon art, of large hopes for renewal.

Strikingly, the human action begins in more than disenchantment, in utter fatigue with the Victorian realist's happy ending—marriage. By the time we meet the still young Henchard, he has been married for some time, and there is no romance in it. The ideal of the hearth, of the limited but satisfying life to which Dickens led his protagonists, in which Adam Bede resolves his career, has turned bitter. The married couple are not at home and content, but on the road and wearily out of touch with each other. We are here beyond the point to which George Eliot takes us when she begins *Middlemarch* with the fated marriage of Dorothea and Casaubon. For Hardy is not engaged in exploring the process by which marital ideals dissolve into sullen separateness and bitter disappointment. That is part of the progress of realism, to be sure. But Hardy begins with the given—with the assumption that marriage is bitterly disappointing and imprisoning. And that assumption, one might note, casts a suspicious shadow over the happy marriage between Farfrae and Elizabeth-Jane, with which the novel concludes.

Yet the scene is narrated with a realist's tender care for precision, an almost awkward quest for authenticity, which seduces us into trusting the narrator. Henchard, for example, is described as a man of "fine figure, swarthy, and stern in aspect; and he showed in profile a facial angle so slightly inclined as to be almost perpendicular." The language struggles to place the characters and define them against recognizable nonliterary categories, and implies that the narrator has a wide familiarity with the ways of agrarian laborers. He notes a typical "sullen silence," apparently bred of familiarity, between man and the woman. He describes Henchard's "measured, springless walk," which distinguishes him as a "skilled country man" rather than as a "general laborer." Later, he describes the furmity tent with the particularity customary to the realist: "At the upper end stood a stove, containing a charcoal fire, over which hung a large three-legged crock, sufficiently polished round the rim to show that it was made of bell metal." The narrator's omniscience is restrained: without entering the minds of his characters he implies a wise familiarity with their ways of thought and feeling: "But there was more in that tent than met the cursory glance; and the man, with the instinct of a perverse character, scented it quickly." Later, we are told that the "conversation took a high turn, as it often does on such occasions." Everything implies a quiet, worldly-wise narration of a story growing out of and repeating a thousand such untold stories buried in history, and whose connections with life outside the fiction will be constantly suggested. Peasant wisdom and bluntness mix with the larger historically saddened intelligence of the narrator. Yet within moments we discover that these devices have been working to force our acceptance of Henchard's sale of Susan: "It has been done elsewhere," says Henchard, "and why not here?"

Just as the scene begins to burst the limits of the conventions of realism, and daringly requires comparison to the abrupt beginning of *King Lear,* so Henchard attempts to free himself from the limiting conditions of his life. Everything noted in the densely particular style suggests that he has been diminished by his context; the sullenness of his relation to a wife who has herself been ground down by "civilization"; the "stale familiarity" of their relationship; the "dogged and cynical indifference" manifest in every movement and feature of the man. As we meet him plodding beside his wife, Henchard is (significantly) reading a ballad sheet, turning from the reality of his intimacy with her to a poet's dream of the uncommon. As he drinks, this partly defeated man is transformed, rising to "serenity," then becoming "jovial," then "argumentative," and finally "the qualities signified by the shape of his face, the occasional clench of his mouth, and the fiery spark of his dark eye, begin to tell in his conduct; he was overbearing —even brilliantly quarrelsome." The latent Henchard, released from the restrictions of convention and responsibility, becomes realized. He asserts the sense of his own power and is longing to be free to exercise it: "I'd challenge England to beat me in the fodder business; and if I were a free man again, I'd be worth a thousand pound before I'd done 't."

In George Eliot, this boast would be deflated immediately, but here the larger wish becomes father to the fact, and the realistically created scene slides into romance in which Henchard is hero. Within a few pages, by a process we are not allowed to observe, Henchard has become mayor of Casterbridge. But he is clearly a man who, however firmly his will keeps him under control (as it keeps him from drinking for twenty-one years), acts outside the limits that confine ordinary people. He seems able to withstand the pressures that impinge on other lives, yet all of his life in reality curls around the monstrous secrets of the sale of his wife. As Frankenstein hides from his monster, attempts to rejoin the community and conceal his great dream and his great mistake, so Henchard hides from the reality so vividly and abruptly rendered in the first scene. All of the novel grows—as all of *Frankenstein* grows—from the narrative of the inevitable reemergence of that hidden fact, that illicit thrust at freedom, into the community in which Henchard seeks to find his peace. And as with Frankenstein, but more richly and complexly, we find that the protagonist in the community is ultimately only reenacting his forbidden scene. In Caster-bridge Henchard seeks with respectability to assert the absolute power of his self over a constricting and contingent world. The pressures he denied at the start avenge themselves on him with a completeness far beyond what the logic of his situation would require. But once set in a world carefully defined in the language of social analysis and historical tradition, once seen in the context of delicate financial and human transactions, Henchard must be destroyed. The man of large feeling and deep need—the hero of romance—cannot survive in the context of a carefully particularized society. Henchard is incapable of compro-mise. Neither success nor failure can be ordinary for him. And since the conventions the novel adopts make failure the only possibility for the largely aspiring man, it must be an extraordinary failure. The novel concentrates on his losses, juxtaposes his large ambitions to the moderate ones of Farfrae, and conspires to keep him from the comforts of the real. Henchard is his fate; and the narrative line transcends the limits of realism by cooperating with Henchard's refusal to compromise. All coincidences conspire to make things worse than the compromising conditions of realism would demand.

In retrospect, one feels, they are not quite coincidences, but Henchard writ large. His domination of the book, uncharacteristic of Hardy's work as a whole, forces us to see his hand—or spirit—everywhere. He evokes all the characters whose coincidental appearances play so important a part in the novel; and with each of these, at some point, he reverses roles. In the third chapter, for example, we learn of Susan and Elizabeth-Jane's search for Henchard, which brings them to Casterbridge and reopens his past; not long before we heard of Henchard's search for them, itself significantly cut short by "a certain shyness of revealing his conduct." Again, Henchard is responsible for persuading Farfrae, who will end the novel as the new mayor of Casterbridge, to remain in the town. Later, Lucetta, who had nursed him in an illness, arrives in order to marry Henchard, and he must repay her kindness and reverse their early relationship. The furmity woman comes to town to expose him and, in the powerful scene in which she is brought to trial before him, she argues: "he's no better than I, and has no right to sit there in judgment upon me." Henchard agrees, "I'm no better than she." Even Jopp, who is responsible for the information leading to the skimmity ride, arrives in town just after Farfrae to take the job that Henchard has offered to Farfrae; by the end, Henchard is living where Jopp lives. Henchard creates the world which is to destroy him—even becomes that world.

The remarkable force of the idea that, as Hardy quotes Novalis, "character is fate" is worked out with a minuteness that seems to translate the whole world of the novel into a psychic landscape. Farfrae's dramatic entrance into the novel, for example, corresponds precisely to the moment when Henchard, defending himself against the demand that he replace the bad wheat he has sold, says "If anybody will tell me how to turn grown wheat into wholesome wheat, I'll take it back with pleasure. But it can't be done." Farfrae arrives and does it; and he stays because of Henchard's overwhelming emotional demands on him: "It's providence!" Farfrae says, "should anyone go against it?" Henchard makes "providence."

More important for a full sense of the daring of Hardy's achievement in his challenge of realist conventions is the way he takes pains to call attention to the creaking mechanics of his novel. It is as though, if we had not noticed how remarkable, unlikely or chancy an event has been, Hardy wants to make sure that we do not find it plausible or commonplace. When Farfrae turns up, the narrator remarks, "He might possibly have passed without stopping at all, or at most for half a minute to glance in at the scene, had not his advent coincided with the discussion on corn and bread; in which event this history had never been enacted." Here Hardy turns what might very well have been taken as a donnée of the plot into a coincidence upon which the whole plot must turn. As the story unfolds, Henchard's impulsive energy can be seen to be responsible for every stage of his eventual self-obliteration. He too impulsively reveals his past to Farfrae; he too intensely punishes Abel Whittle; he too ambitiously tries to outdo Farfrae in setting up a fair for the holidays; he too hastily dismisses Farfrae and too angrily responds to Farfrae's determination to set up his own business; he cuts off the courtship between Farfrae and Elizabeth-Jane though, as the narrator remarks, "one would almost have supposed Henchard to have had policy to see that no better *modus vivendi* could be arrived at with Farfrae than by encouraging him to become his son-in-law." Later he too hastily buys corn and then far too hastily sells it. He opens Susan's letter about Elizabeth-Jane at precisely that moment when being recognized as Elizabeth-Jane's father, "the act he had prefigured for weeks with a thrill of pleasure," was to become "no less than a miserable insipidity. . . . His reinstation of her mother had been chiefly for the girl's sake, and the fruition of the whole scheme was such dust and ashes as this."

The novel even implies that it is Henchard's responsibility that Susan dies. After reading a letter from Lucetta, Henchard says, "Upon my heart and soul, if ever I should be left in a position to carry out that marriage with thee, I *ought* to do it—I *ought* to do it, indeed!" The narrator comments, "The contingency he had in mind was, of course, the death of Mrs. Henchard." And the narrative immediately records the death of Mrs. Henchard. It is this kind of thing—possibly to be described as simple coincidence, possibly to be explained in natural-istic terms—which finally gives to *The Mayor of Casterbridge* its distinctive shape and power. Every detail of the action seems to feed into Henchard's being, and every detail of the text requires that we accept it only if we are willing to accept the extravagant with the plausible, or as part of it.

George Eliot had tried, by subtle allusion and careful elaboration of plot, to make the ordinary reverberate with mythic force. But in

Hardy, sometimes with, sometimes without mythic allusions, the plot itself makes the real mythic. Henchard, the tragic king, responsible both for his kingdom and the sin that blights its wheat and him, must move with ironic absoluteness to death. And the movement toward death is prefigured early. "Why the deuce did I come here!" Henchard asks himself as he finds himself in the place of public execution after he has discovered, because of his refusal to heed the instructions on the envelope, that Elizabeth-Jane is not his daughter. "The momentum of his character knew no patience," the narrator later remarks. That momentum moves him, past all possibility of compromise, to disaster. He is saved from suicide after the skimmity ride only by the magical appearance of his effigy in the water. When the furmity woman returns, Henchard has no instinct toward the deception which would keep his long-held secret quiet. By attempting to kill Farfrae he not only finally alienates the last man who can save him, but makes it impossible for Farfrae to believe him when he attempts to inform Farfrae of Lucetta's illness. Again, his relation to Farfrae is rather like Oedipus's relation to the careful Creon. Thus, since he carelessly gave Jopp Lucetta's letters he is responsible for Lucetta's death in two ways.

Finally, his last two self-assertive acts complete his self-annihilation. He breaks into the royal visit, demanding the recognition which he had lost and forcing another scuffle with Farfrae. And when Newson returns to claim Elizabeth-Jane, Henchard unhesitatingly (driven by those same impulses which led him to sell his wife) asserts that she is dead; his final act of deceit loses for him his last possibility of ordinary survival.

His last acts have about them the quality, not of a modern novel, but of a pagan, religious ritual of self-annihilation. He refuses to plead for himself to Elizabeth-Jane: "Among the many hindrances to such a pleading not the least was this, that he did not sufficiently value himself to lessen his sufferings by strenuous appeal or elaborate argument." Elizabeth-Jane discovers that "it was part of his nature to extenuate nothing, and I live on as one of his own worst accusers." She then goes out to look for Henchard. We find that, to the last, the power of his being draws people after him. Elizabeth-Jane and Farfrae seek him; Abel Whittle against Henchard's command, follows him, and aids him as he can. Henchard walks until he can walk no more and ends in a hovel (the whole scene deliberately and daringly constructed to recall King Lear and Edgar in the storm) by writing his will—and the will wills his total obliteration:

"MICHAEL HENCHARD'S WILL.

"That Elizabeth-Jane Farfrae be not told of my death, or
made to grieve on account of me.
　"& that I be not bury'd in consecrated ground.
　"& that no sexton be asked to toll the bell.
　"& that nobody is wished to see my dead body.
　"& that no murners walk behind me at my funeral.
　"& no flours be planted on my grave.
　"& that no man remember me.
　"to this I put my name.

"Michael Henchard."

The irony of "willing" his self-obliteration is powerful, complex,
and inescapable. Even the putting of his name in upper-case letters
becomes an important part of the effect. For Henchard's last written
words are the name he is asking to obliterate—and boldly imprinted.
The annihilation he asks is in excess of the possible, and so by a won-
derful and moving irony, Henchard effects in death what he always
fell short of in life—the dominance of his name. It is as though Henchard
has stumbled onto the modernist criticism that reminds us of the peculiar status of language. It cannot quite name what it names; it speaks
only of itself. It is a fact in the world, but not a representation of it.
Henchard becomes here the absolute self of the fiction he created of his
life and of the world. He ends, like the late-century writers who had,
in effect, given up on the ideals of the Victorian writers speaking to
their audiences and attempting to move the world. Since he cannot
transform the ideal into the real, he transforms the real into the ideal.

In death, Henchard takes us as far as this novel can to the self-
annihilating consequences of the contradictions and failures of the
realist ideal. But in the last chapters, the narrator finally extends to
Farfrae, that mixed sort of protagonist of realistic fiction, the kind of
irony to which he could have been vulnerable throughout the novel.
Everywhere, of course, Farfrae acts so as to represent a practical alter-
native to Henchard's egoist passion for the absolute. The final complex of alternatives and doublings comes when Henchard arrives at the
wedding feast, like the ancient mariner, an uninvited guest with a
monstrous, Frankensteinian tale he might tell. But he is mute, and
hears instead Donald's voice "giving strong expression to a song of his
dear native country that he loved so well as never to have revisited."
And yet here is Henchard, actually "revisiting" his home, although he

had intended to flee it forever. It is Henchard, not Farfrae, who sen-
timentally leaves the canary; and it is at this point that Farfrae is
described as "not the least indisposed" to try to find Henchard, but
largely because he has never cared enough either to hate or to love him.
For a moment, that is, we can almost say that romance is parodying
realism, that it is, through Hardy, having its revenge on an art that has
attempted to drain all excess from experience and to subject human
nature to the rules of common sense and the inevitable contingencies
of ordinary life.

But the last word in the novel belongs to Elizabeth-Jane, a figure
who does not fit easily into any of the patterns I have been suggesting
apply to the novel, and one who seems rather at home in the world
of realistic conventions that Henchard's narrative implicitly mocks.
Elizabeth-Jane provides the only other perspective from which we see
a large part of the experience, and despite her obvious littleness in
relation to Henchard, she is a character more impressively drawn and
more important than she is generally given credit for. Although she
never surrenders to her impulses or to her needs, she is not, as I have
already suggested, simply a Farfrae. If Farfrae, in supplanting Henchard
in every detail of his life, in fact continues the life of the Henchard who is
excessively sensitive to the demands of respectability, Elizabeth-Jane,
herself entangled in respectability, becomes the most authentic commen-
tator on Henchard's experience. Her heart remains always in hiding. It
stirs momentarily for Henchard's grand misguided attempts at mastery.
But in her quiet submission to the movements of the novel's narrative,
she becomes an expression of the way in which "happiness was but the
occasional episode in a general drama of pain." By accepting this view,
staying protected within the limits of respectability and not rejoicing
too much when good fortune comes, she survives to find "tranquility"
and to forget the Henchard whose death brought her vision. She is the
best sort of realistic audience to a tragic drama.

Her preoccupation with respectability indicates her acceptance of
the limits society imposes on action and on dreams, but with her,
clearly, the acceptance is an act of self-protection. There is something
in Elizabeth-Jane of Hardy's own tentativeness, for while, in Henchard,
Hardy ambitiously projects the passions of a large ego beyond the limits
of conventional fiction, as, one imagines, he himself would have liked
to do, the narrative voice in which he tells the story has something of
Elizabeth-Jane's own reserve, and of the wisdom Elizabeth-Jane has
achieved by the end of the novel. Henchard is Hardy's monstrous

fantasy: but he must, like the monster, be destroyed. Thus, it is through Elizabeth-Jane that Hardy allows us to return to the conventions of realism with a new understanding of their importance and of their tenuousness. Elizabeth-Jane makes us aware that it is not possible any longer to imagine the world as fundamentally accessible to the commonsense structures and language of earlier realists, that behind the veneer of society and quiet movement of ordinary life, there lies the "unforeseen," the continuing pain, the irrational intensities of nature and human nature.

Elizabeth-Jane's ultimate vision is a consequence of the experience of disaster. It embodies the wish in art that Hardy seems to have feared to enact in life. The only way to overcome the "worst" that lies beneath all human experience is to confront it intensely. Ironically, what Elizabeth-Jane arrives at is, in effect, the ideology of realism. She has learned and she teaches "the secret . . . of making limited opportunities endurable; which she deemed to consist in the cunning enlargement, by a species of microscopic treatment, of those minute forms of satisfaction that offer themselves to everybody not in positive pain." We emerge from the world of *The Mayor of Casterbridge,* in which the balances of fictional reality have all been reversed and in which, by the sheer force of narrative intensity, the conventions of realism are found wanting weighed against the monstrous energies of human nature, with a sense that the compromises of realism are after all essential. They do not, we see, adequately describe reality; they are modern disguises of realities that, ironically, belong to far more conventional literature; but they are conditions for our survival. Elizabeth-Jane does not allow herself to feel the pressure of Henchard's selfhood as we feel it in his bold concluding signature. Instead, she sensibly (and realistically) follows Henchard's literal instructions on the grounds "that the man who wrote them meant what he said." But in his life, he had rarely done what he "meant."

Realism survives in Hardy, not as a program for writing fiction, but as a discipline to be learned in the containment of the monstrous and the self-divided energies that make of mankind such an anomaly in a hostile universe.

True Correspondence:
The Mayor of Casterbridge

Bruce Johnson

It may well be that for a writer who had never had any theological sense of a cosmic scheme of value, Christian or otherwise, the ancient folk sense that if Nature cohered in ways beyond man's describing, it nonetheless cohered, was both cosmic enough and value enough. If Hardy was able to create a genuinely tragic figure, it perhaps had to be against this natural background—against this problem of the correspondence. And most likely it had also to be in terms of whatever psychological or psychic faculties were paramount in the modern sensibility—were available in contrast to an ancient rustic sensibility that had created its great monuments to the achieved symbiosis in, say, Mai-Dun (Maiden Castle) or Stonehenge.

These are the imaginative categories with which Hardy approaches *The Mayor of Casterbridge*. Most readers agree that with Henchard, Hardy comes closer to creating genuine tragic stature than with Clym or Eustacia, and that with Jude we have tipped over into recognizably modern pathos rather than tragedy. But it may be more nearly correct to say that the very idea of tragedy finally seems to Hardy one of those nets that neither the ancient builders of Stonehenge nor Tess herself would have cast in the first place. Surely after *The Mayor of Casterbridge* not all his reading in Greek drama can save tragedy for the modern world.

Nevertheless, the ontological inspiration that guides this novel may best be described not as a further exploration of Hardy's sense of

From *True Correspondence: A Phenomenology of Thomas Hardy's Novels.* ©1983 by the Board of Regents of the State of Florida. University Presses of Florida, 1983.

the tragic hero but as a willingness to probe one kind of being in terms of another kind—not simply synaesthesia or even the mixed categories of metaphysical poetry, but a peculiar experimentalism that, by the end of chapter 4, has the reader accepting not only "loaves . . . as flat as toads" (made with Henchard's "growed wheat") but the designation of those loaves as "unprincipled bread": "I've been a wife, and I've been a mother, and I never see such unprincipled bread in Casterbridge as this before." This is the first characteristic of the "new" Henchard that Susan and Elizabeth-Jane encounter on their entry into Casterbridge. And yet it is not unlike the capacity of the old Henchard to unprinciple things, to deny them something of their essence and substitute something of the informing principle of another kind of being. The wife auction has been just such an activity.

It is the "crime" that takes him out of the natural life in the fields and puts him into commercial society. Earlier he had worn "leggings yellow as marigolds, corduroys immaculate as new flax, and a neckerchief like a flower garden." After the wife auction, he enters a world that can make him mayor but can never erase what D. H. Lawrence called the "true correspondence between the material cosmos and the human soul." As John Paterson suggests and as I have shown [elsewhere] throughout his first two great pastoral novels, Hardy, like his follower D. H. Lawrence, sought to expand the significance of his characters beyond "the functions of their merely social values and conditions . . . and to make them participants in some larger non-human drama." The very metaphoric texture of Hardy's prose will often suggest not that some human feature, physical or psychological, is "like" some aspect of Nature (as in John Paterson's example of Tess's "peony mouth" or in nearly every metaphor we have examined thus far [in *True Correspondence*]) but that some larger ontology comprehends both. Hardy intends to expand our understanding of human nature by suggesting that the mainstream of the Victorian novel (with its key image of the web, man in society affecting and affected by the slightest movement of any strand) has led us to forget ancient connections with the nonhuman world.

Thus, the wife auction stands at a symbolic moment in Henchard's life, when he is willing to apply a commercial trope to matters between him and his wife (and between him and his self-image) that are not of that order of being, that are ontologically inappropriate, as, for example, other kinds of violence or even desertion would not have been. The auction signals the triumph of social and commercial signification over the more primitive, even atavistic sources of Henchard's being. Using the commercial trope to carry his feelings, whatever they may be, plunges Henchard out of his native element and into a commercial and social world where the talents of Farfrae will eventually, and with no malice, wear him down and finish him off. His life suggests the danger of allowing a man's social significance to be effectively severed from his nonhuman significance, from the source of his energy in natural forces that are not to be gambled upon in commercial speculation.

To begin the novel with such confusion of ontologies unsettles the "nature," the secure essence, of other things throughout the story. It is almost as though the wife auction in some atavistic way had been blasphemy against the principle that such essences had better not be confused lest all Nature be set askew, decentered so that even names no longer seem to go to the heart of things and begin to lead a vagrant life of their own. To call the bread "unprincipled" is far more than a rustic description intimating that Henchard is unprincipled for having sold the bakers and millers sprouted wheat, or the millers unprincipled for claiming they did not know it had sprouted, or all unprincipled for colluding in the deception (the most unprincipled thing of all). Bread, called symbolic of the transition from Nature to culture by men as different as Claude Lévi-Strauss and Thoreau, has thus been unprincipled as surely as Henchard's wife auction had earlier struck at marriage. We may well remember Thoreau's satire of those who would call yeast the essence of bread and his successive elimination of ingredients in search of a more genuine candidate for the role. Like Hardy, Thoreau was a great seeker of essences; not to know them was, after all, to miss Thoreau's own version of the "true correspondence between the material cosmos and the human soul."

The incident with the bread, the wife auction, and, later, such incidents as Henchard's gambling on the weather are all exquisitely structured to suggest just such confusion. Somehow Susan's initially naive and "meek" belief in the "binding force" of the "transaction" strikes us as morally justified and really no mixing of ontologies at all. Henchard's subsequent pledge to stop drinking for as long as he has already lived (twenty-one years) emphasizes only that his capacity for unprincipling his own life has little to do with his drinking. Liquor may have precipitated the crisis, but within him works the ancient antagonist of the pastoral otium, ambition itself, the aspiring mind. We are once again very much in the presence of Hardy's pastoral *Gestalten,* asking the ancient questions, reexamining the nature of otium, suspecting that it may consist in knowing what things are in their essence and particularly what common being man may share with the "material world."

That Hardy is particularly anxious to see man as anything but a unique mode of being we see upon Henchard's leaving the scene of the crime. Surely there was a part of Hardy that would have relished treating marriage as a mere contract, at least insofar as society forced other emotional and moral aspects of the relationship to conform painfully with that commercial mold. In his fascination with the wife auction (his poring over antique instances of it in county records), it is as though Hardy were saying to society: all right, you covertly regard marriage as a contract and commercial expediency while sanctifying that commercialism as though it were a spiritual thing sanctified by God. Let us bring its commercialism out in the open and, through the hyperbole of the auction, push it to a logical conclusion, or at least to a *reductio ad absurdum.* You will not make its legal and commercial aspect serve its psychological and moral reality, as wise men would; instead, as with Jude, you will allow the legal forms to victimize the psychological reality. So be it. If it is really commercial, let us externalize that essence and epitomize it in the auction. If it is spiritual, let us have no more of this covert commercialism.

The wife auction as a symbol is nicely arranged for the ontological exploration of a social institution as much as it is a complex revelation of Henchard's passing from the roughly georgic and pastoral world to the world of mayors and towns and business. Many of Hardy's symbols are precisely of this borderline variety, poised so that both author and reader may look off into two ontologically different sorts of country.

This mixing of categories is to be seen, then, as a means of gingerly probing the being of things—and certainly as a healthy and creative activity for the author. Within Henchard, however, and without the conscious manipulation that the author can manage for himself, such unprincipling can be tragic. Something of its process may be in the nature of art, but it is a dangerous element in a man's life if he is no artist, and possibly even if he is. When Henchard walks out of the tent, Hardy notes that "the difference between the peacefulness of inferior nature and the wilful hostilities of mankind was very apparent at this place." Yet he immediately remembers that mankind might "some night be innocently sleeping when these quiet objects were raging loud" and includes Henchard's violence and Nature's under the comprehensive ontology of "all terrestrial conditions," which are "intermittent."

That Henchard's hostility has been "wilful" is not sufficient to exclude it from this category. Man's will is no ultimate determinant of ontology for Hardy, and Hardy's motive in this philosophic rumination (really an act of considerable daring) is no less expansive for his view of human nature than, for instance, seeing the sun in Elizabeth-Jane's loosely combed hair as though it were in some mode the same as the sunlight penetrating a hazel copse. There is nothing mystical in either of these perceptions; they are, rather, eloquent proof of Hardy's taste for the immanent reality of both the visual moment in the hazel copse and of a nearly unnameable quality in Elizabeth-Jane. The connection may depend on the most delicate perception of modes of being, but it is not transcendent in any Emersonian or Platonic sense. In some entirely legitimate sense of the word, it is more nearly empirical. As Hardy has said in a note, "In spite of myself I cannot help noticing countenances and tempers in objects of scenery, e.g., trees, hills, houses."

While it is not true that the whole plot of *The Mayor of Casterbridge* consists of the consequences of this auction come back to haunt him, still the novel unfolds a sequence of paradoxes built upon the ontological symbol. The man whom Henchard loves, Farfrae, becomes his commercial rival largely because Henchard, having plunged into the commercial world, will not recognize that it is nonetheless outside his nature. While Henchard deals with a handshake and a "Ye shall hae't," Farfrae writes out contracts and balances books; his talent for romance never impinges on his equal talent for orderly business. He sings nostalgic songs about a Scotland he never particularly wants to see again. He weighs alternatives and is expert in taking into account the feelings of others without really responding to those feelings. In short, he is totally untragic and has been made so in contrast to the self-defeating paradox of Henchard. Farfrae is an uncanny portrait of what might be called, in comparison with the Industrial Revolution, the Managerial Revolution.

Henchard's tragic qualities have been variously described, ranging from a subtle "self-destructive" wish and melancholy need to strip people of their dignity, to a taste for liquor and a simple bad temper that plunges ahead without any long-range sense of consequences. If the wife auction, however, is a clue to the qualities in him that are tragic, we shall need to understand the paradoxes it produces in the subsequent action of the novel. Susan becomes a true wife to a man whose legal wife she can never be. She returns to a Henchard whose legal wife she is but with feelings and a child that in every sense belong to Newson. The auction creates a situation where there can be no further correspondence between social form and emotional content. Henchard, like some of Joseph Conrad's characters, has committed a "crime" which has jolted things out of their customary significations and made us wonder, indeed, whether even names have anything intrinsic to do with what they are supposed to designate in the social and material world.

Especially Elizabeth-Jane sees the world in this seminal disorder as she sits the death watch beside her mother's bed. She is, after all, the victim of so many of these dislocations and dissociations. She hears

> the timepiece in the bedroom ticking frantically against the clock on the stairs [two orderly measures of time and "reality" disagreeing stubbornly with one another]; ticking harder and harder till it seemed to clang like a gong; and all this while the subtle-souled girl asking herself why she was born, why sitting in a room, and blinking at the candle; why things around her had taken the shape they wore in preference to every other possible shape. Why they stared at her so helplessly, as if waiting for the touch of some wand that should release them from terrestrial constraint; what that chaos called consciousness which spun in her at this moment like a top, tended to, and began in. Her eyes fell together; she was awake, yet she was asleep.

As Susan dies, she attempts to designate every detail of her funeral (down to the pennies on her dead eyes), to thrust Elizabeth-Jane into Farfrae's care, and in general to control all the details of existence that Elizabeth-Jane feels are about to spin out of their named and accustomed categories.

Yet the world, especially as it seems to exist after Henchard's crime, will not tolerate such management, any more than Elizabeth-Jane's name or the weather at harvest time will. Confronting Elizabeth-Jane with his desire to change and thereby manage her name, Henchard says, " 'Twas I that chose your name, my daughter; your mother wanted it Susan. There, don't forget 'twas I gave you your name!" But if in Hardy's world names are manipulated, essences cannot be, and Henchard has invited the wrath of the nonexistent gods in his bit of hubris.

Elizabeth-Jane, anxious to stop the ontological spinning mentioned earlier, says, "If it is my name I must have it, mustn't I," and Henchard, anxious to disguise the role of his own will in the matter says, "Well, well;

image is everything in these matters." Of course no sooner is the notice to the newspapers dictated than Henchard goes upstairs to find evidence of her name and discovers Susan's letter saying that Elizabeth-Jane is Newson's child. When, after an anguished walk that night, he returns to his newly named daughter, who is no daughter, ironically he finds an Elizabeth-Jane who from this moment on calls him father and nearly becomes his emotional child. This kind of irony concerning the identity of things and people is fundamental to *The Mayor of Casterbridge*.

Henchard creates his own fate by denying "the true correspondence between the material cosmos and the human soul," by cutting himself off from a genius for such symbiosis in the sense of not recognizing the wellspring of his true temperamental power. But he nonetheless dies having disappeared as though "he had sunk into the earth," on the borders of the Ishmaelite Egdon Heath and among the tumuli of the earliest tribes, tombs which look like the breasts of "Diana Multimammia fully extended there." In his death the connection is reaffirmed. Farfrae may interpose harvesting and planting machines between the primordial sower and reaper and their connection with the very soil they turn, but Farfrae has nothing to lose in the way of that true correspondence: his temperament is modulated by rational considerations that Great Mother knows nothing of. She is tempestuous or tranquil in the passionate manner of a Greek god. And in Henchard, Hardy has phenomenologically caught this quality; it is the key to both his stature—as it is Lear's—and his fall.

Visual Appearance and Psychological Reality in *The Mayor of Casterbridge*

J. B. Bullen

> *"It is a man's sincerity and* depth of vision *that make him a poet."*
>
> *"The gifted man is he who* sees *the essential point, and leaves all the rest aside as surplusage."*
>
> *"Penetrate through obscurity and confusion to seize the characteristic features of an object."*
>
> THOMAS CARLYLE, "The Hero as Poet," Hardy's emphasis

When, in the autumn of 1880, Hardy reached chapter 13 of *A Laodicean,* he fell ill, and the remainder of the novel had to be dictated from his bed. He was not happy with the result, and ascribed the failure of the book, at least in part, to his living in London. "Residence in or near a city," he claimed, "tended to force mechanical and ordinary production from his pen." So in the next few years he set about trying to find a location better suited to his temperament. First, he and his wife went to Wimbourne in Dorset, where they rented a house and Hardy began writing *Two on a Tower*. The move was not a success, and, according to Hardy's biographer Michael Millgate, the couple failed to become integrated into the local community. This book, too, was less than successful. It was written hurriedly and never received Hardy's full attention, and even before he had finished it, he felt that he had "lost his way" as a novelist. Neither *A Laodicean* nor *Two on a Tower* had been

From *The Expressive Eye: Fiction and Perception in the Work of Thomas Hardy.* ©1986 by J. B. Bullen. Oxford University Press, 1986.

shaped by Hardy's intuition. Each is dominated by abstract ideas, and the settings, which had played such a successful and important part in his earlier work, had become far-flung and exotic. What he needed, he said, was "an ample theme," but one which was related to "the intense interests [and] passions . . . that throb through the commonest lives." He was quite right, and eventually the pursuit of the commonplace brought him back to the scenes of his childhood and youth; in 1883 he and Emma moved back to the Borough of Dorchester.

There is no doubt that one of the strengths of *The Mayor of Caster-bridge* is the conviction with which Hardy portrays Wessex provincial life. The richness of the texture of that life comes principally from Hardy's sharp eye for detail, and from his feel for the social structures of small-town existence. In *A Laodicean* and *Two on a Tower,* idea took precedence over image, so the characters remained flat and their lives shadowy. In *The Mayor of Casterbridge* the ideological patterning is more carefully hidden, and is never allowed to assume greater importance than narrative or character. This is achieved in part through a proliferation of visual detail and in part through Hardy's unwavering attention to the significance of observed phenomena. Casterbridge itself, for example, is seen from all angles. As Susan Henchard and Elizabeth-Jane approach it for the first time, Hardy presents the little community, not only from afar and close to, but also from above:

> To birds of the more soaring kind Casterbridge must have appeared on this fine evening as a mosaic-work of subdued reds, browns, greys, and crystals, held together by a rectangular frame of deep green. To the level eye of humanity it stood as an indistinct mass behind a dense stockade of limes and chestnuts, set in the midst of miles of rotund down and concave field.

This sense of a strong, physical presence extends even to the smallest details of Casterbridge life. When Elizabeth-Jane visits Michael Henchard, the furnishings of his room are rendered with a similar conviction.

> The dining-room to which he introduced her still exhibited the remnants of the lavish breakfast laid for Farfrae. It was furnished to profusion with heavy mahogany furniture of the deepest red-Spanish hues. Pembroke tables, with leaves hanging so low that they well-nigh touched the floor, stood against the walls on legs and feet shaped like those of an

elephant, and on one lay three huge folio volumes—a Family Bible, a "Josephus," and a "Whole Duty of Man."

There is no doubt that Hardy's move to Dorchester played a major part in the development of this style of writing. Not only did he involve himself in Dorchester society and renew his interest in local traditions and customs, but there was one event above all others which helped him rediscover his creative roots. After years of wandering about the country, he found a permanent residence which served to express his personality and embody many of his aspirations.

Almost as soon as Hardy moved to Dorchester, he made up his mind to build a house. From a temporary residence in Shire-Hall Place, he began negotiations with the Duchy of Cornwall for a one-and-a-half-acre site on the outskirts of the town. By November 1883 the well had been dug, the trees planted, and the foundations laid out. The symbolic significance of this house is hard to overstate. For Hardy, who had always lived in rented accommodation, such a dwelling was a monument to his success; but what is even more important is that the design itself was entirely his own. The physical labour was carried out by his father and brother, but Hardy oversaw everything from the foundations to the roof; he was responsible for the details of the plumbing and the layout of the heating; he decided on the disposition and construction of the windows and doors; and he even supervised the planting of the garden. It was as if his life, which had previously been so rootless and nebulous, suddenly materialized in bricks, mortar, and stone.

It comes as no surprise to learn that the building of Max Gate coincides exactly with the writing of *The Mayor of Casterbridge*. The mornings would be spent constructing piece by piece the material life of fictional Casterbridge, and in the afternoons Hardy would be intimately involved with the paraphernalia of building. Just as the form of the novel took shape in Hardy's mind, so his new house rose before his eyes.

The influence of material things—their design, shape, and colour—can be felt everywhere in *The Mayor of Casterbridge*. No other novel by Hardy presents the physical constituents of life so vividly. From the feel and texture of garments to the design of furniture and interiors, from the details of agricultural implements to the shape and quality of building materials, the text is filled with references to utilitarian and decorative objects. Yet it would be quite wrong to assume that Hardy had merely transcribed what he saw around him, or that he had abandoned abstract issues and ontological concerns. He never looked upon himself as a realist, and stressed that Casterbridge was in no way a replica of Dorchester. "Casterbridge," he said, when he was offered the freedom of the Borough of Dorchester in 1910, "is not Dorchester—not even Dorchester as it existed sixty years ago." Rather, he had taken many liberties with its "ancient walls, streets, and precincts" to create "a dream-place that never was outside an irresponsible book." Yet at the same time he argued for an imaginative connection between life and fiction: "When somebody said to me that 'Casterbridge' is a sort of essence of the town as it used to be, 'a place more Dorchester than Dorchester itself,' I could not absolutely contradict him," and to explain the nature of this "dream-place," Hardy concluded with a visual metaphor: "At any rate," he said, "it is not a photograph in words." The figure of speech is important in defining Hardy's techniques in *The Mayor of Casterbridge,* because it relates to two statements which he made when he was writing the novel. In the first he said that the activity of a novelist is like "looking at a carpet," where, "by following one colour a certain pattern is suggested, by following another colour, another." This process, he said, though it is "quite accurately, a going to Nature" is not a mimetic act, because the result "is no mere photograph, but purely the product of the writer's own mind." The second statement also involves a visual reference, and helps to define even more precisely the way in which Hardy envisaged the process of transformation from the literal to the imaginative. Not long after he had finished writing *The Mayor of Casterbridge,* he wrote in his diary that "his art" was "to intensify the expression of things, as is done by Crivelli, Bellini, etc., so that the heart and inner meaning is made vividly visible."

The Pictorial Analogue

To understand what Hardy meant by this, and its relevance to *The Mayor of Casterbridge,* it is necessary to know what the work of Crivelli and Bellini meant to his contemporaries. Hardy was most familiar with the examples of their painting in the National Gallery—Crivelli's *Pietà* and Bellini's *Agony in the Garden,* for example—and undoubtedly he knew of the way in which they both appeared as transitional figures in contemporary art history. According to the authorities, Bellini inherited something of the harshness of Mantegna's style, yet at the same time anticipated "the golden age of Venetian colourists." The words "sharp" and "primitive" occur frequently in the accounts of Bellini's works, and Crowe and Cavalcaselle claimed that the "sculptural aspect" of the drapery in *The Agony in the Garden* "display[s] much of Mantegna's spirit." This suggestion of a simple, but forceful, expressiveness attached itself even more strongly to the work of Crivelli. He might have created some of "the rudest and most unattractive pictures in art," said Sir Henry Layard, yet other paintings border on "the grandest character." Above all, said Layard, though his forms are often grotesque, his paintings are never "expressionless," and R. N. Wornum said something very similar when he pointed out that though Crivelli's pictures are often "exceedingly hard" and "almost invariably ugly," they never "want expression." Crivelli's paintings, said Crowe and Cavalcaselle, invariably surprise the spectator "by the life which he concentrated into their action and expression."

It is this recurrent word "expression" which is so important, since Hardy, too, wished to "intensify the expression of things." What Crivelli and Bellini did was to transform the natural world and the human body into expressive images—images which expressed the peculiar temperaments of their creators. They managed, through the intensity of their gaze, to find a "beauty in ugliness," to change inert natural form and fill it with personal meaning.

In *The Mayor of Casterbridge* Hardy also endows his images with expressive life. He observes and transcribes the features of Victorian Dorchester in such a way that they partake of a significance which is greater than that apparent on their surface; Hardy manages to reveal the "heart and inner meaning" of things by visible means, and though his model is not directly the painting of Crivelli or Bellini, pictorialism features prominently in bringing the salient features of his images to the mental eye of the reader. This is nowhere clearer than in the opening sequences of the book. The first scene appears at first to be a straightforward rural episode—three travellers on the road to Weydon-Priors—but the manner in which Hardy accounts for the episode suggests not so much a directly observed event as an image in art.

> One evening of late summer, before the nineteenth century had reached one-third of its span, a young man and woman, the latter carrying a child, were approaching the large village of Weydon-Priors, in Upper Wessex, on foot. They were plainly but not ill clad, though the thick hoar of dust which had accumulated on their shoes and garments from

an obviously long journey lent a disadvantageous shabbiness to their appearance just now.

The whole stress of this passage lies on externals and their significance; the narrator assumes the role of a passive and ignorant spectator scanning the image before him for its meaning. He notices the way in which the figures are grouped on the highway, shifts his viewpoint, moves in closer, and reinterprets what he sees. "They walked side by side in such a way as to suggest afar off the low, easy, confidential chat of people full of reciprocity; but on closer view it could be discerned that the man was reading." The static, pictorial quality of the image is enhanced by the use of a technical vocabulary. It is the eye of the draughtsman that sees the anonymous male figure in "profile," with "a facial angle so slightly inclined as to be almost perpendicular"; and it is the eye of the painter which perceives the female face as flesh lit by sunlight when she "caught slantwise the rays of the strongly coloured sun, which made transparencies of her eyelids and nostrils and set fire on her lips." The vagueness of the landscape—it is a place which "might have been matched at almost any spot in any county in England" —and the anonymous road, reminiscent of the "dull uninteresting road" of Mangiarelli's *Near Porta Salara,* serve to strengthen the focus on the central figures. But what emerges most prominently from this opening passage is the appearance of the male figure, and particularly the details of his clothing and the tools of his trade:

> He wore a short jacket of brown corduroy, newer than the remainder of his suit, which was a fustian waistcoat with white horn buttons, breeches of the same, tanned leggings, and a straw hat overlaid with black glazed canvas. At his back he carried by a looped strap a rush basket, from which protruded at one end the crutch of a hay-knife, a wimble for hay-bonds being also visible in the aperture.

Once again in Hardy's work we have an image derived from the genre study of rural life, but its use in this context is quite distinct from the genre paintings of *Under the Greenwood Tree.* In the earlier novel, the static, pictorial quality of the scenes was comic in its effect, and was frequently employed to illustrate the sociability of rustic life. Here, the manifold details of the image are charged with secondary meaning, and are expressive of much more than were the pictures of Mellstock society. The differences between the pictorialism of *Under the Greenwood Tree* and that of *The Mayor of Casterbridge* can be illustrated with reference to Thomas Webster's *The Village Choir* and Sir Hubert von Herkomer's picture *Hard Times*. As Christopher Wood suggests, *The Village Choir* could well "illustrate the easy-going eccentricity that survived in rural parishes," and Hardy's text, too, stresses the jovial eccentricity of English rural life. Herkomer's picture is quite different, however, in both technique and effect. It was painted in 1885, just after Hardy had written *The Mayor of Casterbridge,* and though it was not the model for Hardy's opening scene, there are striking similarities. The grouping of the figures is suggestive of their respective mental attitudes—the weariness of the woman and child and the stoicism of the man. Like Henchard, the male figure is unemployed, and the tools of his trade (here thrown down at the side of the road) make his occupation clear, and in both picture and text the clothing of the figures speaks of hardship and penury. In the Herkomer painting, as well as in Hardy's account of the three travellers, all the information is communicated through the visual presentation of physical objects. In Hardy's opening scene, and elsewhere in *The Mayor of Casterbridge,* objects—the material stuff of life—are vested with an importance and a significance which is far greater than their superficial appearance. The rush basket, hay-knife, and curious "wimble" certainly lend an authenticity to the picture of rural life, but, more important, they serve to define very precisely Henchard's occupation in life and his social standing in the rural community. Even more dramatically, his character, personality, and disposition are announced not in any conscious mode of self-expression, but rather in his manner of walking, which in turn is "made visible" in the simple folds in his trousers:

> His measured, springless walk was the walk of the skilled countryman as distinct from the desultory shamble of the general labourer; while in the turn and plant of each foot there was, further, a dogged and cynical indifference personal to himself, showing its presence even in the regularly interchanging fustian folds, now in the left leg, now in the right, as he paced along.

Henchard's clothing and the tools of his trade serve to establish the primary relationship between the visual and the conceptual in *The Mayor of Casterbridge.* At one level the novel is about the meaning of clothing—not just the garments which man places on his body, but the objects with which he surrounds himself, which in their turn consciously or unconsciously express his inner nature. Hardy's primary source for the idea is Carlyle, and particularly Carlyle's investigation of the "world in clothes" in *Sartor Resartus*, but he may also have known about the theories of Gottfried Semper, who stressed the idea that all the physical extensions of *Homo sapiens*, from simple forms of ornament to the most elaborate architectural structures, are essentially an expression of man's spirit.

THE METAPHORICAL FUNCTION OF CLOTHING

Henchard's hay-knife, "wimble," leggings, waistcoat, and breeches all recur towards the end of *The Mayor of Casterbridge*. When Henchard leaves the town for the last time, he vainly tries to reestablish his former identity by cleaning up his "old hay-knife and wimble," setting himself up in "fresh leggings, knee-naps and corduroys," and once again the narrator adopts the pictorial mode. "Though she [Elizabeth-Jane] did not know it Henchard formed at this moment much the same *picture* as he had presented when entering Casterbridge for the first time nearly a quarter of a century before" (my emphasis). It is against the opening picture that Henchard's changing appearance is constantly measured. After a gap of sixteen years Susan sees her former husband dining in the Kings Arms at Casterbridge, and immediately that original image asserts itself in her mind. "When last she had seen him he was sitting in a corduroy jacket, fustian waistcoat and breeches and tanned leather leggings, with a basin of hot furmity before him." Now, the "old-fashioned evening suit [and] an expanse of frilled shirt" announce Henchard's new-found fortune, and the "heavy gold chain" eloquently proclaims his status; but his subsequent fall from respectability is accompanied by a further series of sartorial changes. When he begs to be allowed to participate in the reception for the Prince of Wales, his petition to the Council is conducted in "the very clothes which he had used to wear in the primal days when he had sat among them," though those clothes are now "frayed and threadbare." Even when he appears in the Royal Presence, he clings pathetically to the trappings of his former status, "doggedly [retaining] the fretted and weather-beaten garments of bygone years." And when, towards the end of the novel, Henchard takes on the work of general labourer, his image as skilled countryman again reasserts itself in the text. He once wore "clean, suitable clothes, light and cheerful in hue; leggings yellow as marigolds, corduroys immaculate as new flax, and a neckerchief like a flower garden"—emblems of simplicity, dignity, and naturalness—but in his fallen state "he wore the remains of an old blue cloth suit of his gentlemanly times, a rusty silk hat, and a once black satin stock, soiled and shabby."

The changes which take place in Henchard's appearance as a result of his shifting status are unconscious ones, and his attitude to clothing, like his attitude to most things, is spontaneous and unpremeditated. This is not true of all the characters in the novel, many of whom are acutely conscious of their appearance. Within the text, the discussion of fashions, the numerous references to details of dress, and the persistent allusions to the sartorial appearance of other characters act as a constant reminder to the reader that clothing here has a significance which lies beyond appearances. The two most important characters in this respect are undoubtedly Elizabeth-Jane and Lucetta Templeman, and both their similarities and their differences focus specifically on their respective attitudes to dress and clothing and, in consequence, to the larger issues of appearance and reality.

Elizabeth-Jane first comes to Casterbridge as part of her mother's plan to free them from what Hardy (in an undoubtedly self-conscious metaphor) calls "the strait-waistcoat of poverty." It is no accident that her entry into the novel, which takes place on "the highroad to Weydon-Priors," reproduces many of the features of the very first "picture" of the novel, and focuses sharply on matters of dress. Susan Henchard "was dressed in the mourning clothes of a widow. Her companion, also in black, appeared as a well-formed young woman of about eighteen." Under the auspices of Henchard, Elizabeth-Jane and her mother prosper, and that prosperity is marked by outward changes. "It might have been supposed," says the narrator, "that. . . a girl rapidly becoming . . . comfortably circumstanced. . . would go and make a fool of herself by dress," but Elizabeth-Jane formed instead "curious resolves on checking gay fancies in the matter of clothes." A momentary lapse in those resolves, however, provides an important clue to the central position which clothes occupy in this novel. One day Henchard gave Elizabeth-Jane some "delicately tinted" gloves:

> She wanted to wear them to show her appreciation of his kindness, but she had no bonnet that would harmonize. As an artistic indulgence she thought she would have such a bonnet. When she had a bonnet that would go with the gloves she had no dress that would go with the bonnet. It was now absolutely necessary to finish; she ordered the requisite article, and found that she had no sunshade to go

with the dress. In for a penny, in for a pound; she bought the sunshade, and the whole structure was at last complete.

The "structure," or artefact, which Elizabeth-Jane creates is not the natural expression of her personality, but the result of "an artistic indulgence," and its effect on those around her is dramatic and immediate. She becomes "visible" to the inhabitants of Casterbridge, who, "as soon as [they] thought her artful. . .thought her worth notice," and when even Donald Farfrae is moved by her appearance, Elizabeth-Jane decides to recreate the same structure before the mirror to test its effect. Putting on the "muslin, the spencer, the sandals, [and] the parasol," she looked at her reflection. What she sees, however, is not her real self but "a picture"—a false image: "The *picture* glassed back was, in her opinion, precisely of such a kind as to inspire that fleeting regard, and no more" (my emphasis). Unlike most women, whose eyes, says the narrator in a cynical aside, are "ruled. . .so largely by the superficies of things"—one thinks of Bathsheba Everdene in this context—Elizabeth-Jane is conscious of the discrepancy between her inner self and the artefact which she has created. This is important, since throughout *The Mayor of Casterbridge,* "art"—whether it is the art of the fashion-designer or even the skill of the painter—is always associated with "artfulness," with false appearances, personal cunning, and ultimately moral duplicity, and Elizabeth-Jane's clear-sightedness in these matters is emphasized by contrast with that "artful little woman" Lucetta Templeman.

Lucetta enters the story as Elizabeth-Jane's doppelgänger. Like Elizabeth-Jane on the road to Weydon-Priors, "the personage was in mourning. . .was about her age and size, and she might have been her wraith or double, but for the fact that it was a lady much more beautifully dressed than she." It is significant that Elizabeth-Jane's eyes "were arrested by the artistic perfection of the lady's appearance," since that "artistic appearance" is to play an important part in Lucetta's development as a character vis-à-vis Elizabeth-Jane. Lucetta is a complete "art-work," and her faith in the value of appearances is her undoing. In a passage which Hardy subsequently deleted from the manuscript, he makes this very clear—probably too clear for his purposes. When Elizabeth-Jane first visits Lucetta, she asks her, "How did you know the way to dress so well?" Lucetta explains how she bought and paid for her appearance:

I went to Paris to the largest Magazin, and said, "Make me

serves him for a lingering one; finally, he leaves Casterbridge to all appearances the double of the figure who entered it. Many of these replicas are created through similarities of sartorial appearance; the images look alike because they are dressed alike, and, as Penelope Vigar suggests, throughout the story, "details of dress and appearance are made to function both as overt representations of character, and as symbolic commentary on the novel's theme." Lucetta believes that garments express a meaning which can be manipulated by artifice, but she is unable to read the "inner meaning" of their forms. Elsewhere, Abel Whittle's breeches provide the immediate cause of the first major struggle between Henchard and Farfrae; Elizabeth-Jane's expensive muff tells Henchard that a new relationship has been struck up between Farfrae and her; and when Henchard leaves Casterbridge for the last time, he takes with him some "cast-off belongings" of Elizabeth-Jane "in the shape of gloves [and] shoes." Throughout the novel clothing acts as a means of recording both personal and communal life. Even a detail like the state of the furmity woman's apron expresses the changes in her personal fortunes. She was "once thriving [and] cleanly white aproned," but returns to the story in "a shawl of that nameless tertiary hue which comes, but cannot be made." At the communal level, the life of the Casterbridge townsfolk can be read in their garments. The marketplace, says the narrator, is "a little world of leggings, switches and sample bags," where "suits . . . were the historical records of their wearers' deeds . . . and daily struggles for many years past."

Consequently, clothes and clothing in *The Mayor of Casterbridge* have a double role. As visual objects they impart to the narrative a sense of materiality; their form, substance, design, and texture lend a palpability to the character of their wearers, and communicate a strong sense of the quotidian and the commonplace. But clothes are also highly symbolic in their nature, and each of the sartorial details points to aspects of character or social status which are essentially intangible and abstract in quality. In this way, not only is the daily life of Casterbridge communicated through the physical objects which constitute that life, but those same objects express some of the moral values, aspirations, and ambitions of the inhabitants of the town. Casterbridge is literally a "world in clothes," and the metaphorical use which Hardy makes of the material substance of Casterbridge life strongly resembles the ideas of another writer who attached great importance to the symbolic function of dress. This was, of course, Thomas Carlyle, who, in *Sartor Resartus* of 1833, claimed, through the words of his imaginary Professor

fashionable," holding out some bank-note
stripped me, and put on me what they chose.
hovered round me, fixed me on a pedestal like a
arranged me and pinned me and stitched me and
When it was over I told them to send several mo
the same size, and so it was done.

In the final version of the novel, two dresses arrive
Hall, not from Paris but from London, and Lucetta
the bed in the form of two "images," each suggesting
Her choice between them is a measure of the differ
between herself and Elizabeth-Jane: " 'You are that po
to one of the arrangements), 'or you are *that* totally d
(pointing to the other) 'for the whole of the coming sp
Elizabeth-Jane, Lucetta believes that clothes makes th
Lucetta's misplaced faith in the value of appearances is
cause of her death. As Penelope Vigar points out, "Lu
vanity is parodied by the bawdy fantasy of the skimmi
blazons noisily and 'with lurid distinctness' the scandal
relationship with Michael Henchard." "How folk do
clothes," comments one of the jealous and disaffected r
another, Nance Mockridge by name, would "like to see t
pulled of such Christmas candles" as Lucetta. Carefully dres
of Lucetta and Henchard are paraded back to back in a sec
gänger episode. The figure of Lucetta is "dressed as *she* was d
she sat in the front seat at the time the play-actors came t
Hall," exclaims one of the spectators of the skimmity-ride;
uncovered, and her hair in bands, and her back-comb in pla
on a puce silk, and white stockings, and coloured shoes." F
time Lucetta sees herself as she really is, and reality breaks tl
pearance. "She's me—she's me—even to the parasol—my g
sol," cries the bewildered girl, and unable to stand so much r
into a paroxysm from which she never recovers.

The "double" is extremely important in *The Mayor of C*
in pointing up the discrepancy between illusions of all kind
often cruel nature of reality which those illusions conceal. E
Jane is herself the double of her dead stepsister; the living
is a replica of the Newson supposed dead; and Henchard hir
his doubles. His own image floats before him in the weir at
Hatches. It prevents the quick death he is planning for him

fashionable," holding out some bank-notes. They half stripped me, and put on me what they chose. Four women hovered round me, fixed me on a pedestal like an image, and arranged me and pinned me and stitched me and padded me. When it was over I told them to send several more dresses of the same size, and so it was done.

In the final version of the novel, two dresses arrived at High Place Hall, not from Paris but from London, and Lucetta spreads them on the bed in the form of two "images," each suggesting a human figure. Her choice between them is a measure of the difference in attitude between herself and Elizabeth-Jane: " 'You are that person' (pointing to one of the arrangements), 'or you are *that* totally different person' (pointing to the other) 'for the whole of the coming spring.' " Unlike Elizabeth-Jane, Lucetta believes that clothes makes the woman, and Lucetta's misplaced faith in the value of appearances is the immediate cause of her death. As Penelope Vigar points out, "Lucetta's flimsy vanity is parodied by the bawdy fantasy of the skimmity-ride which blazons noisily and 'with lurid distinctness' the scandal of her former relationship with Michael Henchard." "How folk do worship fine clothes," comments one of the jealous and disaffected rustics, while another, Nance Mockridge by name, would "like to see the trimming pulled of such Christmas candles" as Lucetta. Carefully dressed "images" of Lucetta and Henchard are paraded back to back in a second doppel-gänger episode. The figure of Lucetta is "dressed as *she* was dressed when she sat in the front seat at the time the play-actors came to the Town Hall," exclaims one of the spectators of the skimmity-ride; "her neck is uncovered, and her hair in bands, and her back-comb in place; she's got on a puce silk, and white stockings, and coloured shoes." For the first time Lucetta sees herself as she really is, and reality breaks through ap-pearance. "She's me—she's me—even to the parasol—my green para-sol," cries the bewildered girl, and unable to stand so much reality, falls into a paroxysm from which she never recovers.

The "double" is extremely important in *The Mayor of Casterbridge* in pointing up the discrepancy between illusions of all kinds and the often cruel nature of reality which those illusions conceal. Elizabeth-Jane is herself the double of her dead stepsister; the living Newson is a replica of the Newson supposed dead; and Henchard himself has his doubles. His own image floats before him in the weir at the Ten Hatches. It prevents the quick death he is planning for himself and preserves him for a lingering one; finally, he leaves Casterbridge to all appearances the double of the figure who entered it. Many of these replicas are created through similarities of sartorial appearance; the images look alike because they are dressed alike, and, as Penelope Vigar suggests, throughout the story, "details of dress and appearance are made to function both as overt representations of character, and as a symbolic commentary on the novel's theme." Lucetta believes that garments express a meaning which can be manipulated by artifice, but she is unable to read the "inner meaning" of their forms. Elsewhere, Abel Whittle's breeches provide the immediate cause of the first major struggle between Henchard and Farfrae; Elizabeth-Jane's expensive muff tells Henchard that a new relationship has been struck up between Farfrae and her; and when Henchard leaves Casterbridge for the last time, he takes with him some "cast-off belongings" of Elizabeth-Jane "in the shape of gloves [and] shoes." Throughout the novel clothing acts as a means of recording both personal and communal life. Even a detail like the state of the furmity woman's apron expresses the changes in her personal fortunes. She was "once thriving [and] cleanly white aproned," but returns to the story in "a shawl of that nameless tertiary hue which comes, but cannot be made." At the communal level, the life of the Casterbridge townsfolk can be read in their garments. The marketplace, says the narrator, is "a little world of leggings, switches and sample bags," where "suits . . . were the historical records of their wearers' deeds . . . and daily struggles for many years past."

Consequently, clothes and clothing in *The Mayor of Casterbridge* have a double role. As visual objects they impart to the narrative a sense of materiality; their form, substance, design, and texture lend a palpability to the character of their wearers, and communicate a strong sense of the quotidian and the commonplace. But clothes are also highly symbolic in their nature, and each of the sartorial details points to aspects of character or social status which are essentially intangible and abstract in quality. In this way, not only is the daily life of Casterbridge communicated through the physical objects which constitute that life, but those same objects express some of the moral values, aspirations, and ambitions of the inhabitants of the town. Casterbridge is literally a "world in clothes," and the metaphorical use which Hardy makes of the material substance of Casterbridge life strongly resembles the ideas of another writer who attached great importance to the symbolic function of dress. This was, of course, Thomas Carlyle, who, in *Sartor Resartus* of 1833, claimed, through the words of his imaginary Professor

Teufelsdröckh, that, "clothes, as despicable as we think them, are so unspeakably significant." *Sartor Resartus* is an extended investigation and analysis of this central idea, and throughout the book Carlyle uses the metaphor of clothing to explore the relationship between appearance and reality in human life. "Men," says Carlyle,

> are properly said to be clothed with Authority, clothed with Beauty, with Curses, and the like. Nay, if you consider it, what is Man himself, and his whole terrestrial Life, but an Emblem; a Clothing or visible Garment for that devine ME of his, cast hither, like a light-particle, down from Heaven?

According to Carlyle, clothing has both a utilitarian and an expressive role in the life of the individual. On the one hand, as "the tatters raked from the Charnel-house of Nature," clothing covers his brute nakedness, but on the other, it acts as the symbolic expression of his spirit. "Clothes," he says, "gave us individuality, distinctions, social polity; Clothes have made Men of us." But if we are unaware of the distinction between reality and mere appearance, he says, or are deceived into taking the garment for the man, then clothes will "make Clothesscreens of us."

Though Hardy's admiration for Carlyle was qualified, Carlyle remained a powerful influence throughout his life. He often read and reread his copy of Carlyle's *Works,* and *Sartor Resartus* was one of his favourite texts. He alludes to it in his account of Egdon Heath in *The Return of the Native,* where the "venerable one coat" of the heath provides a "satire on human vanity in clothes," and when asked by the editor of the *Fortnightly Review* to nominate a favourite passage of prose for an article "Fine Passages in Verse and Prose, Selected by Living Men of Letters," Hardy chose something from *Sartor Resartus.*

In both *Sartor Resartus* and *The Mayor of Casterbridge,* clothing is an emblem of man's status among his fellows. *"Man,"* says Carlyle, *"is a Spirit . . . bound by invisible bonds to All Men,"* and his clothes are "the visible emblems of that fact." "Society," he adds, "is founded upon cloth"; "clothes . . . are like a tissue woven by men as an emblem of the connection between them." In *The Mayor of Casterbridge* Henchard's massive gold chain is a symbol of his standing in society; he is, as Carlyle put it, "clothed with Authority." Yet Carlyle warns just how ephemeral and insubstantial such symbols can be. "On a sudden," he says, "as by some enchanter's wand . . . the Clothes fly-off . . . and Dukes, Grandees, Bishops, Generals, Annointed Presence itself . . . stand straddling there, not a shirt on them." Henchard's chain of authority is similarly insubstantial; he violates the socially accepted bond between himself and his wife, he is stripped of his chain and his other symbols of office, and his own nakedness is suggestively prefigured in his insistence that Abel Whittle should apear at work *sans culottes.*

Though *Sartor Resartus* starts out as a disquisition on clothes and clothing, as it progresses, Carlyle expands and extends the meaning of these words to take in much more than the materials that adorn the body. He conceives of the body itself as a form of clothing for the spirit; furthermore, in the physical world all those objects which man creates and uses— his tools, his furnishings, his buildings, his very towns and cities—fall under Carlyle's definition of clothing, each being the symbolic expression of man's inner nature. In *The Mayor of Casterbridge* Hardy employs a similar principle. Take tools, for example. The prominence of tools—the hay-knife and "wimble"—in the first picture of Henchard has already been pointed out, and it is those same tools which he "refurbishes" when he leaves Casterbridge. "Man," Carlyle points out, "is a Tool-using Animal."

> Weak in himself, and of small stature, he stands on a basis, at most for the flattest-soled, of some half-square foot, insecurely enough. . . . Nevertheless he can use Tools, can devise Tools . . . without Tools he is nothing, with Tools he is all.

The inhabitants of Casterbridge realize that "without Tools they are nothing," and the shop windows of the town proclaim the importance of implements. There were

> scythes, reap-hooks, sheep-shears, bill-hooks, spades, mattocks, and hoes at the iron-monger's; bee-hives, butter-firkins, churns, milking stools and pails, hay-rakes, field-flagons, and seed-lips at the cooper's; cart-ropes and plough-harness at the saddler's; carts, wheelbarrows, and mill-gear at the wheelwright's and machinist's; horse-embrocations at the chemist's; at the glover's and leather cutter's, hedging-gloves, thatchers' kneecaps, ploughmen's leggings, villagers' patterns and clogs.

This list, which Hardy says is "endless," is much more than a picturesque detail. The elaborate gear and tackle embody a whole way of life, rich and diverse. It is a traditional, old-fashioned life, and the plethora of tools which symbolize it stands in marked contrast to the single piece of machinery which appears so starkly one day in Casterbridge market-square—Farfrae's horse-drill. "It was," says Hardy, "[a] new-fashioned agricultural implement...till then unknown, in its modern shape, in this part of the country." It is a vivid object whose primary and secondary colours are quite unlike the tertiary hues of Casterbridge. There is also a hint about it of the unnatural and the grotesque. "The machine," says Hardy, "was painted in bright hues of green, yellow, and red, and it resembled as a whole a compound of hornet, grasshopper, and shrimp, magnified enormously." The implements in the shop windows are the product of a slow and natural evolution; the horse-drill is emphatically the creation of an age of machinery. Between the two there is both gain and loss. Carlyle speaks ironically of the great "progress" man has made in "the interval between the first wooden Dibble fashioned by man, and those Liverpool Steam-carriages," and Hardy suggests that with the advent of newfangledness, "the rugged picturesqueness of the old method disappeared with its inconveniences." In the text of the novel, the literal depiction of tools merges with their symbolic significance. When, for example, Farfrae takes over the corn trade, his new and ferocious efficiency is expressed through the instruments of measurement: "The scales and steelyards began to be busy where guess-work had formerly been the rule," while at an even more metaphorical level, the conflict between Farfrae and Henchard is likened to the opposition between primitive instruments. "It was," says Hardy, "the dirk against the cudgel."

In *Sartor Resartus,* Carlyle, in the persona of Professor Teufelsdröckh, observes the "clothing" of man's existence from a double perspective. Sometimes it is the substantial projection of man's spirit; at other times it is ephemeral and phantasmagoric. On some occasions Teufelsdröckh sees "clothing" as charged with inner significance. He looks "into the mystery of the World; recognising in the highest sensible phenomena...fresh or faded raiment," observing that "all objects are as windows, through which the philosophic eye looks into Infinitude itself." Yet at other times the professor declares that material things are illusive, and that "a whole immensity of Brussels carpets, and pier-glasses, and or-molu...cannot hide from me that such Drawing-room is simply a section of Infinite space." The substantial and the palpable melt into nothingness, and "we sit in a boundless Phantasmagoria and Dream-grotto [where]...sounds and many-coloured visions flit round our sense." A very similar dualism operates in *The Mayor of Casterbridge.* Elizabeth-Jane, for example, is sensitive to the true significance of appearances, and to the way in which outward appearances can convey inner meaning, yet she, like Teufelsdröckh, is troubled by the insubstantiality of material existence. As she nurses her dying mother,

> the subtle-souled girl [was] asking herself why she was born, why sitting in a room, and blinking at the candle; why things around her had taken the shape they wore in preference to every other possible shape. Why they stared at her so helplessly, as if waiting for the touch of some wand that should release them from terrestrial constraint; what that chaos called consciousness, which spun in her at this moment like a top, tended to, and began in.

"In that strange Dream," says Teufelsdröckh, "how we clutch at shadows as if they were substances; and sleep deepest while fancying ourselves most awake." Similarly, as Elizabeth-Jane contemplates the insubstantiality of things, "her eyes fell together; she was awake, yet she was asleep."

The events of *The Mayor of Casterbridge* lend support to Elizabeth-Jane's anxiety about "the wand" which might touch material things and "release them from terrestrial constraint," or, in Carlyle's words, the "enchanter's wand" which makes the clothes "fly-off," reducing man to a naked animal. Henchard, for example, surrounds himself with objects which reflect a solid, substantial way of life. His belongings are massive in the simple, physical sense. The "profusion [of] . . . heavy mahogany furniture of the deepest red-Spanish hues," the "Pembroke tables, with leaves hanging so low that they well-nigh touched the floor" and "with legs and feet shaped like those of an elephant," together with the "lofty" rooms and "wide" landings of his house all contribute to the illusion of permanence and size. In his account of Henchard's belongings, Hardy dwells on visual details, using images in which antiquity and affluence mingle to create an aura of timeless stability: "the old pier-glass, with gilt columns and huge entablature, the picture-frames, sundry knobs and handles, and the brass rosette at the bottom of each riband bell-pull on either side of the chimney-piece." Carlyle had warned against trusting to "a whole immensity of Brussels carpets, and pier-glasses and ormolu," and sure enough, the certainties of Henchard's life are destroyed as if by supernatural agency: "Like Prester John's, his table had been spread, and infernal harpies had snatched up the food." The mayoral chain passes to Farfrae, who not only moves into Henchard's house, but also marries the woman whom Henchard had assumed was his. Appropriately, it is Henchard's furniture which most vividly symbolizes his ruin. Farfrae buys it all, then offers a few pieces to the former mayor as a gift.

The play on the relationship between the substantial and the illusory extends to other interior scenes in the novel. Lucetta, for example, creates an elaborate setting for herself at High Place Hall which is a reflection of her "artfulness." In contrast to the dark and massive objects in the mayor's house, the light and airy High Place Hall is "prettily furnished." The "little square piano with brass inlayings" and the "sofa with two cylindrical pillows" speak of an advanced taste in furnishings. "I didn't know such furniture as this could be bought in Casterbridge," says Henchard, who is more familiar with Pembroke tables and pier-glasses. "Nor can it be," replies Lucetta, "nor will it till fifty years more of civilization have passed over the town." When Henchard describes Lucetta as "an artful little woman," he means that she is cunning, but, as we have seen, the word also implies that she is the creator and manipulator of artifice. The inhabitants of Casterbridge wrongly thought that Elizabeth-Jane was "artful" when she dressed brilliantly, but the term is in fact totally appropriate for Lucetta. Not only is she someone who gazes upon Casterbridge life "as a picture merely," she actually strikes poses reminiscent of famous works of art. On the occasion of Elizabeth-Jane's visit to High Place Hall, Lucetta "deposited herself on the sofa in. . . [a] flexuous position, and throwing her arm above her brow—somewhat in the pose of a well-known conception of Titian's—talked up at Elizabeth-Jane invertedly across her forehead and arm." Hardy may well have seen Titian's *Rape of Europa* which was shown at the Academy in 1876 and Lord Sutherland's *Diana and Acteon*. He may have been thinking of *Jupiter and Antiope,* otherwise known as the *Pardo Venus* which he would have seen in the Louvre, for each of them employs this distinctive pose. In both the *Diana* and the *Pardo Venus* the mythological females recline seductively in attitudes of languid sexuality, and in both they are being "discovered" by prospective lovers. When Lucetta thinks that she, too, might receive a male visitor, she prepares to be similarly "discovered." Giving orders that any gentleman should be admitted to her room immediately,

she arranged herself picturesquely in the chair; first this way, then that; next so that the light fell over her head. Next she flung herself on the couch in the cyma-recta curve which so became her, and with her arm over the brow looked towards the door.

Lucetta is no more a real Diana, however, than Farfrae is a real Acteon, and, hearing footsteps on the stair, Lucetta, "forgetting her curve (for Nature was too strong for Art as yet), jumped up and ran and hid herself behind one of the window-curtains in a freak of timidity." In *Desperate Remedies* Cytherea Graye's "masterpiece of movement" is modelled on Greuze's *Head of a Girl,* and in *A Pair of Blue Eyes* Elfride Swancourt appears to Stephen Smith like the picture of a saint from a medieval painting, but both Cytherea and Elfride adopt poses spontaneously and unconsciously. Lucetta Templeman is obsessed with appearances, however, and like George Eliot's Gwendolen Harleth, she is fully aware of her stylized attitudes. "How do I appear to people?" she asks Elizabeth-Jane. "Well—a little worn," replies the astute girl, and treating her friend more in the spirit of art than life, eyes her "as a critic eyes a doubtful painting."

Lucetta also tries to arrange the lives of others according to the dictates of art, and her particular "masterpiece" forms one of the most curious episodes in the novel. Henchard and Farfrae, who are both courting her, are invited to tea at High Place Hall. The atmosphere is formal and frigid, and the studied artifice is modelled this time not on Titian, but on early Italian art.

> They sat stiffly side by side at the darkening table, like some Tuscan painting of the two disciples supping at Emmaus. Lucetta, forming the third and haloed figure, was opposite them; Elizabeth-Jane, being out of the game, and out of the group, could observe all from afar, like the evangelist who had to write it down.

Though the analogy with painting is not Lucetta's but the narrator's, the unnatural stiffness of the image forms an integral part of the artifice with which Lucetta surrounds herself. The whole episode has been carefully engineered by Lucetta, and the frozen formality of what she has created contrasts strongly with the sounds that the four protagonists hear through the windows of High Place Hall. Inside, all is reduced to stasis, and is perceived through the eye; outside the vitality of life is experienced through the ear, as they hear

> the click of a heel on the pavement under the window, the passing of a wheelbarrow or cart, the whistling of the carter,

the gush of water into householder's buckets at the town-pump opposite; the exchange of greetings among their neighbours, and the rattle of the yokes by which they carried off their evening supply.

Elizabeth-Jane is the passive spectator of all this, "the evangelist who had to write it down." She watches as Henchard courts Lucetta, and is forced to watch when Lucetta shifts her affection to Farfrae. She is the most speculative and philosophical member of Casterbridge society, and in this respect is not unlike Professor Teufelsdröckh. But just as Henchard and Lucetta create interiors expressive of their character, so Elizabeth-Jane inhabits rooms which reflect her temperament, and it is surely no coincidence that those rooms resemble in certain important respects Teufelsdröckh's accommodation. The professor inhabits a "speculum or watch-tower" from which "he might see the whole life-circulation of [his] considerable City"; similarly, Elizabeth-Jane's room in Henchard's house was "rather high . . . so that it . . . afforded her opportunity for accurate observation." With Lucetta by her side, she surveys the town from another vantage-point—a window in High Place Hall—and what is merely "a picture" for Lucetta is full of human meaning for Elizabeth-Jane as she explains the identity of each of the townsfolk. Elizabeth-Jane's final lodgings are also located on high. She takes an "upper room no larger than the Prophet's chamber . . . nearly opposite her stepfather's former residence," from which she can see "Donald and Lucetta speeding in and out of the door."

There are correspondences, too, between the meditative activity of Teufelsdröckh and Elizabeth-Jane and the furnishings of their vantage-points. The professor's "Wahngasse watch-tower" "was a strange apartment; full of books and tattered papers, and miscellaneous shreds of all conceivable substances. . . . Books lay on tables, and below tables." Though Elizabeth-Jane is a much tidier creature, she, too, spends "hours . . . devoted to studying such books as she could get hold of." When she moves to join Henchard in his seed and grain shop, she creates another "Prophet's chamber" characteristic of her desire for learning. Henchard strays in one day, and "what struck him about it was the abundance of books lying everywhere. Their number and quality made the meagre furniture that supported them seem absurdly disproportionate." Elizabeth-Jane's furniture is "meagre," and Henchard's is substantial and has all the appearance of permanence, whereas Lucetta's is a small collection of lightweight artworks. All these furnishings, however, fall into the category of "clothing" in Carlyle's definition of the term. Henchard, with his naive belief in the permanence of things, resembles Carlyle's noble but naked anthropophagus who fails to distinguish between appearance and reality; Lucetta is Carlyle's "clothes-screen," for whom life is a matter of externals or a series of self-conscious artifices. Only Elizabeth-Jane, from "the crystalline sphere of a straightforward mind," is fully aware of the significance of the material world, and can interpret the language of "clothes." She alone perceives their true symbolic import, and she alone refuses to encumber her life with what is ultimately ephemeral. But in *The Mayor of Casterbridge,* the clothes metaphor does not rest here; it is not confined to those aspects of material life over which men and women have decisive control. It extends to include the structure of Casterbridge itself—its houses, buildings, inns, and taverns—and extends even to the design of the town, the special topographical features of which are expressive of the lives of its inhabitants past and present.

Chronology

1840	Thomas Hardy is born on June 2 in Higher Bockhampton, a community in the parish of Stinsford, Dorset. He is the son of Thomas Hardy, a stone mason, and Jemima Hand Hardy.
1848	Begins his education at a school in Lower Bockhampton.
1849	Hardy is moved to a school in Dorchester.
1855	Begins teaching at the Stinsford Church Sunday School.
1856	Hardy is accepted at the office of architect John Hicks as pupil. Also in this year Hardy meets Horace Moule and William Barnes.
ca. 1860	Hardy writes his first poem, "Domicilium."
1862	After settling in London, Hardy goes to work for architect and church restorer Arthur Blomfield. He reads widely, studies paintings at the National Gallery, and becomes an agnostic.
1863	The Royal Institute of British Architects awards Hardy an essay prize.
1865	*Chambers' Journal* publishes "How I Built Myself a House." Hardy attends French classes at King's College, Cambridge.
1867	Hardy returns to Dorset and resumes working for John Hicks. At this time, he also begins work on his first novel, *The Poor Man and the Lady.*
1868	*The Poor Man and the Lady* is rejected by Macmillan; Hardy resubmits the manuscript to Chapman & Hall.
1869	Hardy meets George Meredith. Begins his second novel, *Desperate Remedies.*
1870	Hardy travels to Cornwall, where he meets Emma

Lavinia Gifford, his future wife. Publisher William Tinsley agrees to produce *Desperate Remedies* at the author's expense.

1871   *Desperate Remedies* published. Also in this year Hardy writes *Under the Greenwood Tree* and begins *A Pair of Blue Eyes.*

1872   *Under the Greenwood Tree* published. *A Pair of Blue Eyes* appears in serial form.

1873   Hardy's friend Horace Moule commits suicide. Hardy is invited by Leslie Stephen to contribute to *Cornhill;* Hardy then begins the serialized version of *Far from the Madding Crowd. A Pair of Blue Eyes* published.

1874   *Far from the Madding Crowd* published. Hardy marries Emma Lavinia Gifford; they travel to France after the wedding, and upon return settle in Surbiton.

1876   *The Hand of Ethelberta* appears. Hardy and his wife travel to Holland and Germany, and then move to a home at Sturminster Newton, in Dorset.

1878   *The Return of the Native* published. Hardy moves once again, to London, where he is elected to the Savile Club.

1879   Hardy pursues research for *The Trumpet-Major* in the British Museum.

1880   *The Trumpet-Major* published. Hardy meets the Poet Laureate, Alfred, Lord Tennyson. The writing of *A Laodicean* is slowed by a serious illness.

1881   *A Laodicean* published.

1882   *Two on a Tower* published.

1883   Hardy moves to Dorchester, where he begins building his home, Max Gate. "The Dorsetshire Labourer" appears in *Longman's Magazine.*

1884   Hardy begins composition of *The Mayor of Casterbridge.*

1885   Moves into Max Gate. He starts writing *The Woodlanders.*

1886   *The Mayor of Casterbridge* published.

1887   *The Woodlanders* published. Hardy visits Italy.

1888   *The Wessex Tales,* a collection of short stories, published. Composition of *Tess of the D'Urbervilles* begins.

1889   Several publishers reject the first installments of *Tess.*

1890   Hardy finishes *Tess.*

1891   Both *Tess of the D'Urbervilles* and *A Group of Noble Dames* published.

1892   Hardy's father dies. The first version of *The Well-Beloved* is serialized. Relations with his wife begin to deteriorate, and worsen over the next two years, particularly during the composition of *Jude the Obscure*.

1893   Hardy travels to Dublin and Oxford, where he visits Florence Henniker, with whom he writes a short story, and, it is believed, falls in love.

1894   *Life's Little Ironies,* a collection of poems, published.

1895   *Jude the Obscure* published and receives primarily outraged reviews. As a result Hardy decides to discontinue novel-writing and henceforward produces only poetry. Also in this year Hardy works on the Uniform Edition of his novels.

1897   *The Well-Beloved* published.

1898   Publishes *The Wessex Poems.*

1901   Publishes *Poems of the Past and the Present.*

1904   *The Dynasts,* part 1, published. Hardy's mother dies.

1905   Hardy receives an honorary LL.D. from Aberdeen.

1906   *The Dynasts,* part 2, published.

1908   *The Dynasts,* part 3, published.

1909   Publishes *Time's Laughingstocks.* Hardy becomes the governor of the Dorchester Grammar School.

1910   Hardy is awarded the O.M. (Order of Merit).

1912   Hardy's wife Emma Lavinia dies on November 27.

1913   *A Changed Man* published. Hardy receives an honorary D.Litt. degree from Cambridge; he is also made an honorary Fellow of Magdalen College, Cambridge.

1914   Hardy marries Florence Emily Dugdale. The collection of poems called *Satires of Circumstance* published. As World War I begins Hardy joins a group of writers dedicated to the support of the Allied cause.

1915   Hardy's sister Mary dies.

1917   *Moments of Vision,* a collection of poetry, published.

1919   Hardy's first *Collected Poems* published.

1920   Oxford University awards Hardy an honorary D.Litt.

1921   Publishes *Late Lyrics and Earlier.* Becomes honorary Fellow at Queen's College, Oxford.

1923   *The Famous Tragedy of the Queen of Cornwall* published. Hardy receives a visit from the Prince of Wales at Max Gate.

1925   *Human Shows* published.
1928   Hardy dies on January 11; his ashes are buried at West-
        minster Abbey, and his heart is placed at his first wife's
        grave in the Stinsford churchyard. *Winter Words* pub-
        lished posthumously. Florence Emily Hardy publishes
        The Early Life of Thomas Hardy, believed to have been
        written largely by Hardy himself.
1930   *Collected Poems* published posthumously. Florence
        Emily Hardy publishes *The Later Years of Thomas
        Hardy.*

Contributors

HAROLD BLOOM, Sterling Professor of the Humanities at Yale University, is the author of *The Anxiety of Influence, Poetry and Repression,* and many other volumes of literary criticism. His forthcoming study, *Freud: Transference and Authority,* attempts a full-scale reading of all of Freud's major writings. A MacArthur Prize Fellow, he is general editor of five series of literary criticism published by Chelsea House. During 1987–88, he served as Charles Eliot Norton Professor of Poetry at Harvard University.

BERT G. HORNBACK is Professor of English at the University of Michigan. In addition to *The Metaphor of Chance: Vision and Technique in the Works of Thomas Hardy,* he has written two studies of Dickens and edited the Norton Critical Edition of *Middlemarch.*

IAN GREGOR is Professor of Modern English Literature at the University of Kent. He is the author of several books and has edited a collection of critical essays on the Brontës.

ELAINE SHOWALTER is Professor of English at Princeton University. She is the author of numerous essays, and her books include *A Literature of Their Own: British Women Novelists from Brontë to Lessing.*

GEORGE LEVINE is Professor of English at Rutgers University. He is the author of *The Realistic Imagination* and *The Boundaries of Fiction: Carlyle, Macaulay, Newman* as well as the editor of numerous anthologies on Victorian literature.

BRUCE JOHNSON is Chairman of the English Department at the University of Rochester. He has written on Joseph Conrad (*Conrad's Models of Mind*) as well as extensively on Hardy.

J. B. BULLEN is Lecturer in English at the University of Reading. He has edited Roger Fry's *Vision and Design* and is the author of *The Expressive Eye: Fiction and Perception in the Work of Thomas Hardy.*

Bibliography

Atkins, N. J. *The Country of* The Mayor of Casterbridge. Dorchester, U.K.: The Thomas Hardy Society, 1974.

Bain, Judith. "*The Mayor of Casterbridge*: 'Some Grand Feat of Stagery.' " *South Atlantic Bulletin* 42 (May 1977): 11–22.

Bayley, John. *An Essay on Hardy.* London: Cambridge University Press, 1978.

Bebbington, Brian. "Folksong and Dance in *The Mayor of Casterbridge.*" *English Dance and Song* 40 (Winter 1978): 111, 115.

Bromley, Roger. "The Boundaries of Hegemony: Thomas Hardy and *The Mayor of Casterbridge.*" In *Literature, Society, and the Sociology of Literature. Proceedings of Conference Held at the University of Essex July 1976,* edited by Francis Barker et al., 30–40. Colchester, U.K.: University of Essex Press, 1977.

Brooks, Jean R. *Thomas Hardy: The Poetic Structure.* London: Elek Books, 1971.

Casagrande, Peter J. *Unity in Hardy's Novels: "Repetitive Symmetries."* Lawrence: University Press of Kansas, 1982.

Cox, J. Stevens, ed. *A Thomas Hardy Miscellany.* St. Peter Port, Guernsey: Toucan Press, 1981.

Dave, Jagdish Chandra. *The Human Predicament in Hardy's Novels.* London: Macmillan, 1985.

Davis, W. Eugene and Helmut E. Gerber, comps. and eds. *Thomas Hardy. An Annotated Bibliography of Writings about Him, Volumes I and II.* De Kalb: Northern Illinois University Press, 1983.

Drabble, Margaret, ed. *The Genius of Thomas Hardy.* London: Weidenfeld, 1976.

Draper, Ronald P. "Hardy and Respectability." In *An English Miscellany Presented to W. S. Mackie,* edited by Brian S. Lee, 179–207. London: Oxford University Press, 1977.

———. "*The Mayor of Casterbridge.*" *Critical Quarterly* 25, no. 1 (Spring 1983): 57–70.

———, ed. *Thomas Hardy: The Tragic Novels.* London: Macmillan, 1975.

Eagleton, Terry. "Thomas Hardy: Nature as Language." *Critical Quarterly* 13 no. 2 (Summer 1971): 155–62.

Edwards, Duane D. "*The Mayor of Casterbridge* as Aeschylean Tragedy." *Studies in the Novel* 4 (1972): 608–18.

Elliot, Ralph W. V. *Thomas Hardy's English.* Oxford: Basil Blackwell, 1984.

Enstice, Andrew. *Thomas Hardy: Landscapes of the Mind.* London: Macmillan, 1979.

Firor, Ruth A. *Folkways in Thomas Hardy.* New York: Russell & Russell, 1931.

Fussell, D. H. "The Maladroit Delay: The Changing Times in Thomas Hardy's *Mayor of Casterbridge.*" *Critical Quarterly* 21, no. 3 (1979): 17–30.

Grindle, Juliet M. "Compulsion and Choice in *The Mayor of Casterbridge.*" In *The Novels of Thomas Hardy*, edited by Anne Smith, 91–106. London: Vision, 1979.

Guerard, Albert J. *Thomas Hardy.* Cambridge: Harvard University Press, 1949.

Gundy, Joan. *Hardy and the Sister Arts.* London: Macmillan, 1979.

Hartveit, Lars. *The Art of Persuasion: A Study of Six Novels.* Oslo: Universitetsforlaget, 1977.

Hawkins, Desmond. *Hardy. Novelist and Poet.* New York: Barnes & Noble, 1976.

Hinz, Evelyn. "Hierogamy versus Wedlock: Types of Marriage Plots and Their Relationship to Genres of Prose Fiction." *PMLA* 91 (1976): 900–913.

Hyman, Virginia R. *Ethical Perspective in the Novels of Thomas Hardy.* Port Washington, N.Y.: Kennikat, 1975.

Karl, Frederick R. "*The Mayor of Casterbridge:* A New Fiction Defined—1960, 1975." *Modern Fiction Studies* 21 (1975): 405–28.

Kay-Robinson, Denys. *The Landscape of Thomas Hardy.* Exeter, U.K.: Webb & Bower, 1984.

Kramer, Dale. "Character and the Cycle of Change in *The Mayor of Casterbridge.*" *Tennessee Studies in Literature* 16 (1971): 111–20.

———. *Thomas Hardy: The Forms of Tragedy.* London: Macmillan, 1975.

———, ed. *Critical Approaches to the Fiction of Thomas Hardy.* London: Macmillan, 1979.

Lerner, Laurence. *Thomas Hardy's* The Mayor of Casterbridge: *Tragedy or Social History.* London: Sussex University Press, 1975.

Meisel, Perry. *Thomas Hardy: The Return of the Repressed.* New Haven: Yale University Press, 1972.

Mickelson, Anne Z. *Thomas Hardy's Women and Men: The Defeat of Nature.* Metuchen, N.J.: Scarecrow, 1976.

Migdal, Seymour. "History and Archetype in *The Mayor of Casterbridge.*" *Studies in the Novel* 3 (1971): 284–92.

Miller, Bruce E. "Motives of Annihilation in Hardy's Late Novels." *CLA Journal* 19 (1976): 389–403.

Miller, J. Hillis. *Thomas Hardy: Distance and Desire.* Cambridge: Harvard University Press, 1970.

Millgate, Michael. *Thomas Hardy: A Biography.* New York: Random House, 1982.

———. *Thomas Hardy: His Career as Novelist.* New York: Random House, 1971.

Moore, Kevin Z. "Death against Life: Hardy's Mortified and Mortifying 'Man of Character' in *The Mayor of Casterbridge.*" *Ball State University Forum* 24, no. 3 (1983): 13–25.

Morrell, Roy. "Thomas Hardy and Probability." In *On the Novel: A Present for Walter Allen on His 60th Birthday from His Friends and Colleagues,* edited by B. S. Benedikz, 75–92. London: J. M. Dent, 1971.

Murfin, Ross C. *Swinburne, Hardy, Lawrence and the Burden of Belief.* Chicago: University of Chicago Press, 1978.

Page, Norman. "Hardy's Pictorial Art in *The Mayor of Casterbridge.*" *Etudes Anglaises* 25 (1972): 486–92.

———. *Thomas Hardy.* London: Routledge & Kegan Paul, 1977.

————, ed. *Thomas Hardy. The Writer and His Background*. London: Bell & Hyman, 1980.

Paterson, John. "The Continuing Miracle: Nature and Characters in Thomas Hardy." In *Budmouth Essays on Thomas Hardy, Papers Presented at the 1975 Summer School,* edited by F. B. Pinion. Dorchester, U.K.: The Thomas Hardy Society, 1976.

Peck, John. "Hardy's Novel Endings." *Journal of the Eighteen Nineties Society* 9 (1978): 10–15.

Pinion, F. B. Introduction to *The Mayor of Casterbridge*, by Thomas Hardy. London: Macmillan Education, 1975.

————. *Thomas Hardy: Art and Thought*. London: Macmillan, 1977.

————, ed. *Thomas Hardy and the Modern World*. Dorchester, U.K.: The Thomas Hardy Society, 1974.

Reed, John. *Victorian Conventions*. Athens: Ohio University Press, 1975.

Rogers, Katharine. "Women in Thomas Hardy." *The Centennial Review* 19 (1975): 249–58.

Schwarz, Daniel R. "The Narrator as Character in Hardy's Major Fiction." *Modern Fiction Studies* 18 (1972): 155–72.

Solimine, Joseph. " 'The Turbid Ebb and Flow of Human Misery': 'Love among the Ruins' and *The Mayor of Casterbridge*." *Studies in Browning and His Circle: A Journal of Criticism, History, and Bibliography* 8, no. 2 (1980): 99–101.

Springer, Marlene. *Hardy's Use of Allusion*. Lawrence: University Press of Kansas: 1983.

Starzyk, Lawrence J. "Hardy's *Mayor:* The Antitraditional Basis of Tragedy." *Studies in the Novel* 4 (1972): 592–607.

Stevick, Philip. *The Chapter in Fiction: Theories of Narrative Division*. New York: Syracuse University Press, 1970.

Stewart, J. I. M. *Thomas Hardy: A Critical Biography*. London: Longman Group, 1971.

Sumner, Rosemary. *Thomas Hardy: Psychological Novelist*. London: Macmillan, 1981.

Taft, Michael. "Hardy's Manipulation of Folklore and Literary Imagination: The Case of the Wife Sale in *The Mayor of Casterbridge*." *Studies in the Novel* 13 (1981): 399–407.

Thomas Hardy Annual, 1983–.

Thomas Hardy Society Review, 1975–.

Thomas Hardy Yearbook, 1970–.

Toliver, Harold E. *Pastoral Forms and Attitudes*. Berkeley: University of California Press, 1971.

Vigar, Penelope. *The Novels of Thomas Hardy: Illusion and Reality*. London: Athlone, 1974.

Welsh, Alexander. "Realism as a Practical and Cosmic Joke." *Novel* 9 (1975): 23–39.

Williams, Mervyn. *Thomas Hardy and Rural England*. London: Macmillan, 1972.

Acknowledgments

"The Metaphor of Chance: *The Mayor of Casterbridge* " (originally entitled *"The Mayor of Casterbridge"*) by Bert G. Hornback from *The Metaphor of Chance: Vision and Technique in the Works of Thomas Hardy* by Bert G. Hornback, © 1971 by Bert G. Hornback. Reprinted by permission of Ohio University Press, Athens.

"A Man and His History" (originally entitled "A Man and His History: *The Mayor of Casterbridge* [1880]") by Ian Gregor from *The Great Web: The Form of Hardy's Major Fiction* by Ian Gregor, © 1974 by Ian Gregor. Reprinted by permission of Faber & Faber Ltd.

"The Unmanning of the Mayor of Casterbridge" by Elaine Showalter from *Critical Approaches to the Fiction of Thomas Hardy,* edited by Dale Kramer, © 1979 by Elaine Showalter. Reprinted by permission of Macmillan Press.

"Thomas Hardy's *The Mayor of Casterbridge:* Reversing the Real" by George Levine from *The Realistic Imagination: English Fiction from* Frankenstein *to* Lady Chatterley by George Levine, © 1981 by the University of Chicago. Reprinted by permission of the University of Chicago Press.

"True Correspondence: *The Mayor of Casterbridge*" (originally entitled *"The Mayor of Casterbridge* and *The Woodlanders"*) by Bruce Johnson from *True Correspondence: A Phenomenology of Thomas Hardy's Novels* by Bruce Johnson, © 1983 by the Board of Regents of the State of Florida. Reprinted by permission of the University Presses of Florida.

"Visual Appearance and Psychological Reality in *The Mayor of Casterbridge*" by J. B. Bullen from *The Expressive Eye: Fiction and Perception in the Work of Thomas Hardy* by J. B. Bullen, © 1986 by J. B. Bullen. Reprinted by permission.

Index